CAMBRIDGE LIBRARY COLLECTION

Books of enduring scholarly value

English Men of Letters

In the 1870s, Macmillan publishers began to issue a series of books called 'English Men of Letters' – biographies of English writers by other English writers. The general editor of the series was the journalist, critic, politician, and supporter (and later biographer) of Gladstone, John Morley (1838–1923). The aim was to provide a short introduction to each subject and his works, but also that the life should illuminate the works, and vice versa. The subjects range chronologically from Chaucer to Thackeray and Dickens, and an important feature of the series is that many of the authors (Henry James on Hawthorne, Ward on Dickens) were discussing writers of the previous generation, and some (Trollope on Thackeray) had even known their subjects personally. The series exemplifies the British approach to literary biography and criticism at the end of the nineteenth century, and also reveals which authors were at that time regarded as canonical.

Coleridge

The publication in 1798 of *Lyrical Ballads*, written by William Wordsworth and Samuel Taylor Coleridge (1772–1834), is considered to be the starting point of the Romantic movement. Published in the first series of English Men of Letters in 1884, this biography by H. D. Traill (1842–1900), who also wrote on Sterne for the series, sets Coleridge's work within the context of his troubled childhood, his travels, and the depression and financial crises that plagued his life. The first writer to attempt a detailed account of Coleridge's life and work – which ranged from poetry, journalism and literary criticism to history, philosophy and theology – Traill admits to some difficulty in tracing source material, particularly as Coleridge's theological and philosophical writings were largely incomplete, and remained unpublished at his death. Nonetheless he reveals something of both the writer and also the man famously described by Lamb as 'an Archangel a little damaged'.

Cambridge University Press has long been a pioneer in the reissuing of out-of-print titles from its own backlist, producing digital reprints of books that are still sought after by scholars and students but could not be reprinted economically using traditional technology. The Cambridge Library Collection extends this activity to a wider range of books which are still of importance to researchers and professionals, either for the source material they contain, or as landmarks in the history of their academic discipline.

Drawing from the world-renowned collections in the Cambridge University Library, and guided by the advice of experts in each subject area, Cambridge University Press is using state-of-the-art scanning machines in its own Printing House to capture the content of each book selected for inclusion. The files are processed to give a consistently clear, crisp image, and the books finished to the high quality standard for which the Press is recognised around the world. The latest print-on-demand technology ensures that the books will remain available indefinitely, and that orders for single or multiple copies can quickly be supplied.

The Cambridge Library Collection will bring back to life books of enduring scholarly value (including out-of-copyright works originally issued by other publishers) across a wide range of disciplines in the humanities and social sciences and in science and technology.

Coleridge

HENRY DUFF TRAILL

CAMBRIDGE
UNIVERSITY PRESS

CAMBRIDGE UNIVERSITY PRESS

Cambridge, New York, Melbourne, Madrid, Cape Town,
Singapore, São Paolo, Delhi, Tokyo, Mexico City

Published in the United States of America by Cambridge University Press, New York

www.cambridge.org
Information on this title: www.cambridge.org/9781108034449

© in this compilation Cambridge University Press 2011

This edition first published 1884
This digitally printed version 2011

ISBN 978-1-108-03444-9 Paperback

English Men of Letters

EDITED BY JOHN MORLEY

COLERIDGE

COLERIDGE

BY

H. D. TRAILL

London:

MACMILLAN AND CO.

1884

Printed by R. & R. CLARK, *Edinburgh*.

PREFATORY NOTE.

In a tolerably well-known passage in one of his essays De Quincey enumerates the multiform attainments and powers of Coleridge, and the corresponding varieties of demand made by them on any one who should aspire to become this many-sided man's biographer. The description is slightly touched with the humorous hyperbole characteristic of its author; but it is in substance just, and I cannot but wish that it were possible, within the limits of a preface, to set out the whole of it in excuse for the many inevitable shortcomings of this volume. Having thus made an "exhibit" of it, there would only remain to add that the difficulties with which De Quincey confronts an intending biographer of Coleridge must necessarily be multiplied many-fold by the conditions under which this work is here attempted. No complete biography of Coleridge, at least on any important scale of dimensions, is in existence; no critical appreciation of his work *as a whole*, and as correlated with the circumstances and affected by the changes of his life, has, so far as I am aware, been attempted. To perform either of these two tasks adequately, or even with any approach to adequacy, a writer should at least have the

elbow-room of a portly volume. To attempt the two
together, therefore, and to attempt them within the limits
prescribed to the manuals of this series, is an enterprise which I think should claim, from all at least who
are not offended by its audacity, an almost unbounded
indulgence.

The supply of material for a *Life* of Coleridge is
fairly plentiful, though it is not very easily come by.
For the most part it needs to be hunted up or fished up
—those accustomed to the work will appreciate the
difference between the two processes—from a considerable variety of contemporary documents. Completed
biography of the poet-philosopher there is none, as has
been said, in existence; and the one volume of the
unfinished *Life* left us by Mr. Gillman—a name never
to be mentioned with disrespect, however difficult it may
sometimes be to avoid doing so, by any one who honours
the name and genius of Coleridge—covers, and that in
but a loose and rambling fashion, no more than a few
years. Mr. Cottle's *Recollections of Southey, Wordsworth,
and Coleridge* contains some valuable information on certain points of importance, as also does the *Letters, Conversations, etc., of S. T. C.* by Mr. Allsop. Miss Meteyard's
Group of Eminent Englishmen throws much light on the
relations between Coleridge and his early patrons the
Wedgwoods. Everything, whether critical or biographical, that De Quincey wrote on Coleridgian matters requires, with whatever discount, to be carefully studied.
The Life of Wordsworth, by the Bishop of St. Andrews;
The Correspondence of Southey; the Rev. Derwent Coleridge's brief account of his father's life and writings;
and the prefatory memoir prefixed to the 1880 edition

of Coleridge's *Poetical and Dramatic Works*, have all had
to be consulted. But, after all, there remain several
tantalising gaps in Coleridge's life which refuse to be
bridged over; and one cannot but think that there must
be enough unpublished matter in the possession of his
relatives and the representatives of his friends and cor-
respondents to enable some at least, though doubtless
not all, of these missing links to be supplied. Perhaps
upon a fitting occasion and for an adequate purpose
these materials would be forthcoming.

CONTENTS.

CRITICAL PERIOD.

CHAPTER IV.

1799–1800.

CHAPTER V.

1800–1804.

CHAPTER VI.

1806–1809.

CHAPTER VII.

1809–1810.

CHAPTER VIII.

1810–1816.

METAPHYSICAL AND THEOLOGICAL PERIOD.

CHAPTER IX.

1816–1818.

CHAPTER X.

1818–1834.

CHAPTER XI.

CHAPTER XII.

COLERIDGE.

CHAPTER I.

Birth, parentage, and early years—Christ's Hospital—Jesus College, Cambridge.

[1772-1794.]

ON the 21st of October 1772 there was added to that roll of famous Englishmen of whom Devonshire boasts the parentage a new and not its least illustrious name. SAMUEL TAYLOR COLERIDGE was the son of the Rev. John Coleridge, vicar of Ottery St. Mary in that county, and head master of Henry VIII.'s Free Grammar School in the same town. He was the youngest child of a large family. To the vicar, who had been twice married, his first wife had borne three children, and his second ten. Of these latter, however, one son died in infancy; four others, together with the only daughter of the family, passed away before Samuel had attained his majority; and thus only three of his brothers, James, Edward, and George Coleridge, outlived the eighteenth century. The first of these three survivors became the father of Henry Nelson Coleridge—who married his cousin Sara, the poet's accomplished daughter, and edited his uncle's

Œ   B

posthumous works—and of the late Mr. Justice Coleridge, himself the father of the present Lord Chief-Justice of England. Edward, the second of the three, went, like his eldest brother William, to Pembroke College, Oxford, and like him took orders; and George, also educated at the same college and for the same profession, succeeded eventually to his father's benefice and school. The vicar himself appears from all accounts to have been a man of more mark than most rural incumbents, and probably than a good many schoolmasters of his day. He was a Hebrew scholar of some eminence, and the compiler of a Latin grammar, in which, among other innovations designed to simplify the study of the language for "boys just initiated," he proposed to substitute for the name of "ablative" that of "quale-quare-quidditive case." The mixture of amiable simplicity and not unamiable pedantry to which this stroke of nomenclature testifies was further illustrated in his practice of diversifying his sermons to his village flock with Hebrew quotations, which he always commended to their attention as "the immediate language of the Holy Ghost"—a practice which exposed his successor, himself a learned man, to the complaint of his rustic parishioners, that for all his erudition no "immediate language of the Holy Ghost" was ever to be heard from *him*. On the whole the Rev. John Coleridge appears to have been a gentle and kindly eccentric, whose combination of qualities may have well entitled him to be compared, as his famous son was wont in after-life to compare him, to Parson Adams.

Of the poet's mother we know little; but it is to be gathered from such information as has come to us

through Mr. Gillman from Coleridge himself that, though
reputed to have been a "woman of strong mind," she
exercised less influence on the formation of her son's
mind and character than has frequently been the case
with the not remarkable mothers of remarkable men.
"She was," says Mr. Gillman, " an uneducated woman,
industriously attentive to her household duties, and
devoted to the care of her husband and family. Possessing none even of the most common accomplishments
of her day, she had neither love nor sympathy for the
display of them in others. She disliked, as she would
say, your 'harpsichord ladies,' and strongly tried to
impress upon her sons their little value " (that is, of the
accomplishments) "in their choice of wives." And the
final judgment upon her is that she was "a very good
woman, though, like Martha, over careful in many
things; very ambitious for the advancement of her
sons in life, but wanting, perhaps, that flow of heart
which her husband possessed so largely." Of Coleridge's
boyhood and school-days we are fortunate in being able
to construct an unusually clear and complete idea. Both
from his own autobiographic notes, from the traditionary
testimony of his family, and from the no less valuable
evidence of his most distinguished schoolfellow, we
know that his youthful character and habits assign him
very conspicuously to that perhaps somewhat small class
of eminent men whose boyhood has given distinct
indications of great things to come. Coleridge is as
pronounced a specimen of this class as Scott is of its
opposite. Scott has shown the world how commonplace
a boyhood may precede a maturity of extraordinary
powers. In Coleridge's case a boy of truly extraordinary

qualities was father to one of the most remarkable of
men. As the youngest of ten children (or of thirteen,
reckoning the vicar's family of three by his first wife),
Coleridge attributes the early bent of his disposition to
causes the potency of which one may be permitted to
think that he has somewhat exaggerated. It is not
quite easy to believe that it was only through "certain
jealousies of old Molly," his brother Frank's "dotingly
fond nurse," and the infusions of these jealousies into
his brother's mind, that he was drawn "from life in
motion to life in thought and sensation." The physical
impulses of boyhood, where they exist in vigour, are not
so easily discouraged, and it is probable that they were
naturally weaker and the meditative tendency stronger
than Coleridge in after-life imagined. But to continue:
"I never played," he proceeds, "except by myself, and
then only acting over what I had been reading or fancying, or half one, half the other" (a practice common
enough, it may be remarked, among boys of by no means
morbidly imaginative habit), "cutting down weeds and
nettles with a stick, as one of the seven champions of
Christendom. Alas! I had all the simplicity, all the
docility of the little child, but none of the child's habits.
I never thought as a child—never had the language of
a child." So it fared with him during the period of
his home instruction, the first eight years of his life;
and his father having, as scholar and schoolmaster, no
doubt noted the strange precocity of his youngest son,
appears to have devoted especial attention to his training. "In my ninth year," he continues, "my most
dear, most revered father died suddenly. O that I
might so pass away, if, like him, I were an Israelite with-

out guile. The image of my father, my revered, kind, learned, simple-hearted father, is a religion to me."

Before he had attained his tenth year a presentation to Christ's Hospital was obtained for him by that eminent judge Mr. Justice Buller, a former pupil of his father's; and he was entered at the school on the 18th July 1782. His early bent towards poetry, though it displayed itself in youthful verse of unusual merit, is a less uncommon and arresting characteristic than his precocious speculative activity. Many a raw boy "lisps in numbers, for the numbers come;" but few discourse Alexandrian metaphysics at the same age, for the very good reason that the metaphysics as a rule do not "come." And even among those youths whom curiosity, or more often vanity, induces to dabble in such studies, one would find few indeed over whom they have cast such an irresistible spell as to estrange them for a while from poetry altogether. That this was the experience of Coleridge we have his own words to show. His son and biographer, the Rev. Derwent Coleridge, has a little antedated the poet's stages of development in stating that when his father was sent to Christ's Hospital in his eleventh year he was "already a poet, and yet more characteristically a metaphysician." A poet, yes, and a precocious scholar perhaps to boot, but a metaphysician, no; for "the delightful sketch of him by his friend and schoolfellow Charles Lamb" was pretty evidently taken not at "this period" of his life but some years later. Coleridge's own account of the matter in the *Biographia Literaria*[1] is clear. "At a very premature age, even

[1] He tells us in the *Biographia Literaria* that he had translated the eight hymns of Synesius from the Greek into English

before my fifteenth year," he says, "I had bewildered
myself in metaphysics and in theological controversy.
Nothing else pleased me. History and particular facts
lost all interest in my mind. Poetry (though for a
schoolboy of that age I was above par in English
versification, and had already produced two or three
compositions which I may venture to say were somewhat above mediocrity, and which had gained me more
credit than the sound good sense of my old master was
at all pleased with),—poetry itself, yea, novels and
romance, became insipid to me." He goes on to describe
how highly delighted he was if, during his friendless
wanderings on leave-days, "any passenger, especially if
he were dressed in black," would enter with him into a
conversation, which he soon found the means of directing
to his favourite subject of "providence, foreknowledge,
will, and fate; fixed fate, freewill, foreknowledge absolute."   Undoubtedly it is to this period that one should
refer Lamb's well-known description of "Samuel Taylor
Coleridge, Logician, Metaphysician, Bard."

"How have I seen the casual passer through the cloisters
stand still, entranced with admiration (while he weighed the
disproportion between the speech and the garb of the young
Mirandula), to hear thee unfold in thy deep and sweet
intonations the mysteries of Iamblichus or Plotinus (for even
in those years thou waxedst not pale at such philosophic
draughts), or reciting Homer in the Greek, or Pindar, while
the walls of the old Grey Friars re-echoed with the accents
of the *inspired charity-boy.*"

It is interesting to note such a point as that of the

anacreontics "before his fifteenth year." It is reasonable to suppose,
therefore, that he had more scholarship in 1782 than most boys of
ten years.

"deep and sweet intonations" of the youthful voice—
its most notable and impressive characteristic in after-
life. Another schoolfellow describes the young philosopher as "tall and striking in person, with long black
hair," and as commanding "much deference" among his
schoolfellows. Such was Coleridge between his fifteenth
and seventeenth year, and such continued to be the
state of his mind and the direction of his studies until
he was won back again from what he calls "a pre-
posterous pursuit, injurious to his natural powers and to
the progress of his education," by—it is difficult, even
after the most painstaking study of its explanations, to
record the phenomenon without astonishment—a perusal
of the sonnets of William Lisle Bowles. Deferring,
however, for the present any research into the occult
operation of this converting agency, it will be enough to
note Coleridge's own assurance of its perfect efficacy.
He was completely cured for the time of his metaphysical malady, and "well were it for me perhaps," he
exclaims, "had I never relapsed into the same mental
disease ; if I had continued to pluck the flowers and
reap the harvest from the cultivated surface instead of
delving in the unwholesome quicksilver mines of metaphysic depths." And he goes on to add, in a passage
full of the peculiar melancholy beauty of his prose, and
full too of instruction for the biographer, "But if, in
after-time, I have sought a refuge from bodily pain and
mismanaged sensibility in abstruse researches, which
exercised the strength and subtlety of the understanding
without awakening the feelings of the heart, there was
a long and blessed interval, during which my natural
faculties were allowed to expand and my original

tendencies to develop themselves—my fancy, and the
love of nature, and the sense of beauty in forms and
sounds." This "long and blessed interval" endured, as
we shall see, for some eleven or twelve years.

His own account of his seduction from the paths of
poetry by the wiles of philosophy is that physiology
acted as the go-between. His brother Luke had come
up to London to walk the hospitals, and young
Samuel's insatiable intellectual curiosity immediately
inspired him with a desire to share his brother's pursuit. "Every Saturday I could make or obtain leave,
to the London Hospital trudged I. O! the bliss if I
was permitted to hold the plaisters or attend the dress-
ings. . . . I became wild to be apprenticed to a surgeon ;
English, Latin, yea, Greek books of medicine read I
incessantly. Blanchard's *Latin Medical Dictionary* I had
nearly by heart. Briefly, it was a wild dream, which,
gradually blending with, gradually gave way to, a rage
for metaphysics occasioned by the essays on Liberty and
Necessity in Cato's *Letters*, and more by theology." [1]
At the appointed hour, however, Bowles the emancipator
came, as has been said, to his relief, and having opportunely fallen in love with the eldest daughter of a widow
lady of whose son he had been the patron and protector
at school, we may easily imagine that his liberation from
the spell of metaphysics was complete. "From this time,"
he says, "to my nineteenth year, when I quitted school
for Jesus, Cambridge, was the era of poetry and love."

Of Coleridge's university days we know less ; but the
account of his schoolfellow, Charles Le Grice, accords, so
far as it goes, with what would have been anticipated

[1] Gillman, pp. 22, 23.

from the poet's school life. Although "very studious," and not unambitious of academical honours—within a few months of his entering at Jesus he won the Browne Gold Medal for a Greek Ode on the Slave Trade[1]—his reading, his friend admits, was "desultory and capricious. He took little exercise merely for the sake of exercise, but he was ready at any time to unbend his mind in conversation, and for the sake of this his room was a constant rendezvous of conversation-loving friends. I will not call them loungers, for they did not call to kill time but to enjoy it." From the same record we gather that Coleridge's interest in current politics was already keen, and that he was an eager reader, not only of Burke's famous contributions thereto, but even a devourer of all the pamphlets which swarmed during that agitated period from the press. The desultory student, however, did not altogether intermit his academical studies. In 1793 he competed for another Greek verse prize, this time unsuccessfully. He afterwards described his ode *On Astronomy* as "the finest Greek poem I ever wrote;"[2] but, whatever may have

[1] Of this Coleridge afterwards remarked with justice that its "ideas were better than the language or metre in which they were conveyed." Porson, with little magnanimity, as De Quincey complains, was severe upon its Greek, but its main conception—an appeal to Death to come, a welcome deliverer to the slaves, and to bear them to shores where "they may tell their beloved ones what horrors they, being men, had endured from men"—is moving and effective. De Quincey, however, was undoubtedly right in his opinion that Coleridge's Greek scholarship was not of the exact order. No exact scholar could, for instance, have died in the faith (as Coleridge did) that ἕστησε (S. T. C.) means "he stood," and not "he placed."

[2] Adding "that which gained the prize was contemptible"— an expression of opinion hardly in accordance with Le Grice's

been its merits from the point of view of scholarship, the English translation of it, made eight years after by Southey (in which form alone it now exists), seems hardly to establish its title to the peculiar merit claimed by its author for his earlier effort. The long vacation of this year, spent by him in Devonshire, is also interesting as having given birth to one of the most characteristic of the *Juvenile Poems*, the *Songs of the Pixies*, and the closing months of 1793 were marked by the most singular episode in the poet's earlier career.

It is now perhaps impossible to ascertain whether the cause of this strange adventure of Coleridge's was " chagrin at his disappointment in a love affair " or " a fit of dejection and despondency caused by some debts not amounting to a hundred pounds;" but, actuated by some impulse or other of restless disquietude, Coleridge suddenly quitted Cambridge and came up, very slenderly provided with money, to London, where, after a few days' sojourn, he was compelled by pressure of actual need to enlist, under the name of Silas Titus Comberback[1] (S. T. C.), as a private in the 15th Light Dragoons. It may seem strange to say so, but it strikes one as quite

statement ("Recollections" in *Gentleman's Magazine* for 1836) that "no one was more convinced of the propriety of the decision than Coleridge himself." Mr. Le Grice, however, bears valuable testimony to Coleridge's disappointment, though I think he exaggerates its influence in determining his career.

[1] It is characteristic of the punctilious inaccuracy of Mr. Cottle (*Recollections*, ii. 54) that he should insist that the assumed name was "Cumberbatch, not Comberback," though Coleridge has himself fixed the real name by the jest, "My habits were so little equestrian, that my horse, I doubt not, was of that opinion." This circumstance, though trifling, does not predispose us to accept unquestioningly Mr. Cottle's highly particularised account of Coleridge's experience with his regiment.

conceivable that the world might have been a gainer if fate had kept Coleridge a little longer in the ranks than the four months of his actual service. As it was, however, his military experiences, unlike those of Gibbon, were of no subsequent advantage to him. He was, as he tells us, an execrable rider, a negligent groom of his horse, and, generally, a slack and slovenly trooper; but before drill and discipline had had time to make a smart soldier of him, he chanced to attract the attention of his captain by having written a Latin quotation on the white wall of the stables at Reading. This officer, who it seems was either able to translate the ejaculation, "Eheu! quam infortunii miserrimum est fuisse felicem,"[1] or, at any rate, to recognise the language it was written in, interested himself forthwith on behalf of his scholarly recruit.[2] Coleridge's discharge was obtained at Hounslow on April 10, 1794, and he returned to Cambridge.

The year was destined to be eventful for him in more ways than one. In June he went to Oxford to pay a visit to an old schoolfellow, where an accidental introduction to Robert Southey, then an undergraduate of Balliol, laid the foundation of a friendship destined largely to influence their future lives. In the course of the following August he came to Bristol, where he was met by Southey, and by him introduced to Robert Lovell, through whom and Southey he made the acquaintance of two persons of considerable, if not exactly equal, importance to any young author—his first pub-

---

[1] "In omni adversitate fortunæ, infelicissimum genus est infortunii fuisse felicem."—*Boethius.*

[2] Miss Mitford, in her *Recollections of a Literary Life*, interestingly records the active share taken by her father in procuring the learned trooper's discharge.

lisher and his future wife.   Robert Lovell already knew
Mr. Joseph Cottle, brother of Amos Cottle (Byron's " O !
Amos Cottle ! Phœbus ! what a name "), and himself a
poet of some pretensions ; and he had married Mary
Fricker, one of whose sisters, Edith, was already engaged
to Southey ; while another, Sara, was afterwards to
become Mrs. Coleridge.

As the marriage turned out on the whole an unhappy
one, the present may be a convenient moment for considering how far its future character was determined by
previously existing and unalterable conditions, and how
far it may be regarded as the result of subsequent
events.   De Quincey, whose acute and in many respects
most valuable monograph on the poet touches its
point of least trustworthiness in matters of this kind,
declares roundly, and on the alleged authority of Coleridge himself, that the very primary and essential pre-
requisite of happiness was wanting to the union.
Coleridge, he says, assured him that his marriage was
"not his own deliberate act, but was in a manner forced
upon his sense of honour by the scrupulous Southey,
who insisted that he had gone too far in his attentions
to Miss Fricker for any honourable retreat."   On the
other hand, he adds, " a neutral spectator of the parties
protested to me that if ever in his life he had seen a
man under deep fascination, and what he would have
called desperately in love, Coleridge, in relation to Miss
F., was that man."   One need not, I think, feel much
hesitation in preferring this " neutral spectator's " statement to that of the discontented husband, made several
years after the mutual estrangement of the couple, and
with no great propriety perhaps, to a new acquaintance.

There is abundant evidence in his own poems alone that at the time of, and for at least two or three years subsequently to, his marriage Coleridge's feeling towards his wife was one of profound and indeed of ardent attachment. It is of course quite possible that the passion of so variable, impulsive, and irresolute a temperament as his may have had its hot and cold fits, and that during one of the latter phases Southey may have imagined that his friend needed some such remonstrance as that referred to. But this is not nearly enough to support the assertion that Coleridge's marriage was "in a manner forced upon his sense of honour," and was not his own deliberate act. It was as deliberate as any of his other acts during the years 1794 and 1795,—that is to say, it was as wholly inspired by the enthusiasm of the moment, and as utterly ungoverned by anything in the nature of calculation on the possibilities of the future. He fell in love with Sara Fricker as he fell in love with the French Revolution and with the scheme of "Pantisocracy," and it is indeed extremely probable that the emotions of the lover and the socialist may have subtly acted and reacted upon each other. The Pantisocratic scheme was essentially based at its outset upon a union of kindred souls, for it was clearly necessary of course that each male member of the little community to be founded on the banks of the Susquehanna should take with him a wife. Southey and Lovell had theirs in the persons of two sisters; they were his friends and fellow-workers in the scheme; and they had a sympathetic sister-in-law disengaged. Fate therefore seemed to designate her for Coleridge and with the personal attraction which she no doubt exerted over him there may well have mingled a dash of that mysterious passion for symmetry which prompts a man to "complete the set." After all, too, it must be remembered that, though Mrs. Coleridge did not permanently retain her hold upon her husband's affections, she got considerably the better of those who shared them with her. Coleridge found out the objections to Pantis- ocracy in a very short space of time, and a decided coolness had sprung up between him and Madame la Revolution before another two years had passed.

The whole history indeed of this latter *liaison* is most remarkable, and no one, it seems to me, can hope to form an adequate conception of Coleridge's essential instability of character without bestowing somewhat closer attention upon this passage in his intellectual development than it usually receives. It is not un- common to see the cases of Wordsworth, Southey, and Coleridge lumped together indiscriminately, as inter- equivalent illustrations of the way in which the young and generous minds of that era were first fascinated and then repelled by the French Revolution. As a matter of fact, however, the last of the three cases differed in certain very important respects from the two former. Coleridge not only took the "frenzy-fever" in a more violent form than either Wordsworth or Southey, and uttered wilder things in his delirium than they, but the paroxysm was much shorter, the *immediate* reaction more violent in its effects and brought about by slighter causes in his case than in theirs. This will appear more clearly when we come to contrast the poems of 1794 and 1795 with those of 1797. For the present it must suffice to say that while the history of Coleridge's relations to the French Revolution is intellectually more

interesting than that of Wordsworth's and Southey's, it
plainly indicates, even in that early period of the three
lives, a mind far more at the mercy of essentially transitory sentiment than belonged to either of the others,
and far less disposed than theirs to review the aspirations
of the moment by the steady light of the practical
judgment.

This, however, is anticipating matters. We are still
in the summer of 1794, and we left Coleridge at Bristol
with Southey, Lovell, and the Miss Frickers. To
this year belongs that remarkable experiment in play-
writing at high pressure, *The Fall of Robespierre*. It
originated, we learn from Southey, in " a sportive conversation at poor Lovell's," when each of the three
friends agreed to produce one act of a tragedy, on the
subject indicated in the above title, by the following
evening. Coleridge was to write the first, Southey the
second, and Lovell the third. Southey and Lovell
appeared the next day with their acts complete, Coleridge, characteristically, with only a part of his. Lovell's,
however, was found not to be in keeping with the other
two, so Southey supplied the third as well as the
second, by which time Coleridge had completed the
first. The tragedy was afterwards published entire,
and is usually included in complete editions of Coleridge's poetical works. It is an extremely immature
production, abounding in such coquettings (if nothing
more serious) with bathos as

" Now,
Aloof thou standest from the tottering pillar,
And like a frighted child behind its mother,
Hidest thy pale face in the skirts of Mercy."

and

> " Liberty, condensed awhile, is bursting
> To scatter the arch-chemist in the explosion."

Coleridge also contributed to Southey's *Joan of Arc* certain lines of which, many years afterwards, he wrote in this humorously exaggerated but by no means wholly unjust tone of censure :—" I was really astonished (1) at the schoolboy, wretched, allegoric machinery; (2) at the transmogrification of the fanatic Virago into a modern novel-pawing proselyte of the Age of Reason— a Tom Paine in petticoats; (3) at the utter want of all rhythm in the verse, the monotony and dead plumb-down of the pauses, and at the absence of all bone, muscle, and sinew in the single lines."

In September Coleridge returned to Cambridge, to keep what turned out to be his last term at Jesus. We may fairly suppose that he had already made up his mind to bid adieu to the Alma Mater whose bosom he was about to quit for that of a more venerable and, as he then believed, a gentler mother on the banks of the Susquehanna; but it is not impossible that in any case his departure might have been expedited by the remonstrances of college authority. Dr. Pearce, Master of Jesus, and afterwards Dean of Ely, did all he could, records a friend of a somewhat later date, "to keep him within bounds; but his repeated efforts to reclaim him were to no purpose, and upon one occasion, after a long discussion on the visionary and ruinous tendency of his later schemes, Coleridge cut short the argument by bluntly assuring him, his friend and master, that he mistook the matter altogether. He was neither Jacobin,[1]

---

[1] Carrlyon's *Early Years and late Reflections*, vol. i. p. 27.

he said, nor Democrat, but a Pantisocrat." And, leaving the good doctor to digest this new and strange epithet, Coleridge bade farewell to his college and his university, and went forth into that world with which he was to wage so painful and variable a struggle.

CHAPTER II.

The Bristol Lectures—Marriage—Life at Clevedon—The *Watchman*—Retirement to Stowey—Introduction to Wordsworth.

[1794-1797.]

THE reflections of the worthy Master of Jesus upon the strange reply of the wayward young undergraduate would have been involved in even greater perplexity if he could have looked forward a few months into the future. For after a winter spent in London, and enlivened by those *noctes cœnæque Deûm* at the "Cat and Salutation," which Lamb has so charmingly recorded, Coleridge returned with Southey to Bristol at the beginning of 1795, and there proceeded to deliver a series of lectures which, whatever their other merits, would certainly not have assisted Dr. Pearce to grasp the distinction between a Pantisocrat and a Jacobin. As a scholar and a man of literary taste he might possibly have admired the rhetorical force of the following outburst, but, considering that the "HE" here gibbeted in capitals was no less a personage than the "heaven-born minister" himself, a plain man might well have wondered what additional force the vocabulary of Jacobinism could have infused into the language of Pantisocracy. After summing up the crimes of the Reign of Terror the lecturer asks : "Who, my brethren, was the cause of this guilt if not HE who supplied the occasion and the motive ? Heaven hath bestowed on *that man* a portion of its ubiquity, and given him an actual presence in the sacraments of hell, wherever administered, in all the bread of bitterness, in all the cups of blood." And in general, indeed, the *Conciones ad Populum*, as Coleridge named these lectures on their subsequent publication, were rather calculated to bewilder any of the youthful lecturer's well-wishers who might be anxious for some means of discriminating his attitude from that of the Hardys, the Horne Tookes, and the Thelwalls of the day. A little warmth of language might no doubt be allowed to a young friend of liberty in discussing legislation which, in the retrospect, has staggered even so staunch a Tory as Sir Archibald Alison ; but Coleridge's denunciation of the Pitt and Grenville Acts, in the lecture entitled *The Plot Discovered*, is occasionally startling, even for that day of fierce passions, in the fierceness of its language. It is interesting, however, to note the ever-active play of thought and reasoning amid the very storm and stress of political passion. Coleridge is never for long together a mere declaimer on popular rights and ministerial tyranny, and even this indignant address contains a passage of extremely just and thoughtful analysis of the constituent elements of despotism. Throughout the spring and summer of 1795 Coleridge continued his lectures at Bristol, his head still simmering—though less violently, it may be suspected, every month—with Pantisocracy, and certainly with all his kindred political and religious enthusiasms unabated.

A study of these crude but vigorous addresses reveals to us, as does the earlier of the early poems, a mind struggling with its half-formed and ever-changing conceptions of the world, and, as is usual at such peculiar phases of an intellectual development, affirming its temporary beliefs with a fervour and vehemence directly proportioned to the recency of their birth. Commenting on the *Conciones ad Populum* many years afterwards, and invoking them as witnesses to his political consistency as an author, Coleridge remarked that with the exception of " two or three pages involving the doctrine of philosophical necessity and Unitarianism," he saw little or nothing in these outbursts of his youthful zeal to retract, and, with the exception of " some flame-coloured epithets " applied to persons, as to Mr. Pitt and others, " or rather to personifications "—for such, he says, they really were to him—as little to regret.

We now, however, arrive at an event, important in the life of every man, and which influenced that of Coleridge to an extent not the less certainly extraordinary because difficult, if not impossible, to define with exactitude. On the 4th of October 1795 Coleridge was married at St. Mary Redcliffe Church, Bristol, to Sarah (or as he preferred to spell it Sara) Fricker, and withdrew for a time from the eager intellectual life of a political lecturer to the contemplative quiet appropriate to the honeymoon of a poet, spent in a sequestered cottage amid beautiful scenery, and within sound of the sea. No wonder that among such surroundings, and with such belongings, the honeymoon should have extended from one month to three, and indeed that Coleridge should have waited till his youthful yearnings for a life of

action, and perhaps (though that would have lent itself
less gracefully to his poem of farewell to his Clevedon
cottage) his increasing sense of the necessity of supple-
menting the ambrosia of love with the bread and cheese
of mortals, compelled him to re-enter the world. No
wonder he should have delayed to do so, for it is as easy
to perceive in his poems that these were days of unclouded happiness as it is melancholy to reflect by
how few others like them his life was destined to be
brightened. The *Æolian Harp* has no more than the
moderate merits, with its full share of the characteristic
faults, of his earlier productions; but one cannot help
"reading into it" the poet's after-life of disappointment
and disillusion—estrangement from the "beloved woman"
in whose affection he was then reposing; decay and dis-
appearance of those "flitting phantasies" with which
he was then so joyously trifling, and the bitterly ironical
scholia which fate was preparing for such lines as

"And tranquil muse upon tranquillity."

One cannot in fact refrain from mentally comparing
the *Æolian Harp* of 1795 with the *Dejection* of 1803,
and no one who has thoroughly felt the spirit of
both poems can make that comparison without emotion.
The former piece is not, as has been said, in a literary
sense remarkable. With the exception of the one
point of metrical style, to be touched on presently,
it has almost no note of poetic distinction save
such as belongs of right to any simple record of a
mood which itself forms the highest poetry of the average
man's life; and one well knows whence came the
criticism of that MS. note inscribed by S. T. C. in a

copy of the second edition of his early poems, "This I
think the most perfect poem I ever wrote. Bad may
be the best perhaps." One feels that the annotator
might just as well have written, "How perfect was the
happiness which this poem recalls!" for this is really
all that Coleridge's eulogium, with its touching bias from
the hand of memory, amounts to.

It has become time, however, to speak more generally
of Coleridge's early poems. The peaceful winter months
of 1795-96 were in all likelihood spent in arranging and
revising the products of those poetic impulses which had
more or less actively stirred within him from his seventeenth year upwards ; and in April 1797 there appeared
at Bristol a volume of some fifty pieces entitled *Poems
on Various Subjects, by S. T. Coleridge, late of Jesus
College Cambridge.* It was published by his friend
Cottle, who, in a mixture of the generous with the
speculative instinct, had given him thirty guineas for the
copyright. Its contents are of a miscellaneous kind,
consisting partly of rhymed irregular odes, partly of
a collection of *Sonnets on Eminent Characters,* and partly
(and principally) of a blank verse poem of several
hundred lines, then, and indeed for years afterwards,
regarded by many of the poet's admirers as his masterpiece—the *Religious Musings.*[1]

To the second edition of these poems, which was
published in the following year, Coleridge, at all times a
candid critic (to the limited extent to which it is possible
even for the finest judges to be so) of his own works,
prefixed a preface, wherein he remarks that his poems

---

[1] The volume contained also three sonnets by Charles Lamb,
one of which was destined to have a somewhat curious history.

have been "rightly charged with a profusion of double epithets and a general turgidness," and adds that he has "pruned the double epithets with no sparing hand," and used his best efforts to tame the swell and glitter both of thought and diction. "The latter fault, however, had," he continues, "so insinuated itself into my *Religious Musings* with such intricacy of union that sometimes I have omitted to disentangle the weed from fear of snapping the flower." This is plain-spoken criticism, but I do not think that any reader who is competent to pronounce judgment on the point will be inclined to deprecate its severity. Nay, in order to get done with fault-finding as soon as possible, it must perhaps be added that the admitted turgidness of the poems is often something more than a mere defect of style, and that the verse is turgid because the feeling which it expresses is exaggerated. The "youthful bard unknown to fame" who, in the *Songs of the Pixies*, is made to "heave the gentle misery of a sigh," is only doing a natural thing described in ludicrously and unnaturally stilted terms; but the young admirer of the *Robbers*, who informs Schiller that if he were to meet him in the evening wandering in his loftier mood "beneath some vast old tempest-swinging wood," he would "gaze upon him awhile in mute awe" and then "weep aloud in a wild ecstasy," endangers the reader's gravity not so much by extravagance of diction as by over-effusiveness of sentiment. The former of these two offences differs from the latter by the difference between "fustian" and "gush." And there is, in fact, more frequent exception to be taken to the character of the thought in these poems than to that of the style. The remarkable gift of eloquence, which seems to have belonged to Coleridge from boyhood, tended naturally to aggravate that very common fault of young poets whose faculty of expression has outstripped the growth of their intellectual and emotional experiences—the fault of wordiness. Page after page of the poems of 1796 is filled with what one cannot, on the most favourable terms, rank higher than rhetorical commonplace ; stanza after stanza falls pleasantly upon the ear without suggesting any image sufficiently striking to arrest the eye of the imagination, or awakening any thought sufficiently novel to lay hold upon the mind. The *Æolian Harp* has been already referred to as a pleasing poem, and reading it, as we must, in constant recollection of the circumstances in which it was written, it unquestionably is so. But in none of the descriptions either of external objects or of internal feeling which are to be found in this and its companion piece, the *Reflections on having left a Place of Retirement*, is there anything which can fairly be said to elevate them above the level of graceful verse. It is only in the region of the fantastic and supernatural that Coleridge's imagination, as he was destined to show by a far more splendid example two years afterwards, seems to acquire true poetic distinction. It is in the *Songs of the Pixies* that the young man "heaves the gentle misery of a sigh," and the sympathetic interest of the reader of to-day is chilled by the too frequent intrusion of certain abstract ladies, each preceded by her capital letter and attended by her "adjective-in-waiting ;" but, after all deductions for the conventionalisms of "white-robed Purity," "meek-eyed Pity," "graceful Ease," etc., one cannot but feel that the *Songs of the Pixies* was the off-

spring not of a mere abundant and picturesque vocabulary but of a true poetic fancy. It is worth far more as
an earnest of future achievement than the very unequal
Monody on the Death of Chatterton (for which indeed we
ought to make special allowance, as having been commenced in the author's eighteenth year), and certainly
than anything which could be quoted from the *Effusions*,
as Coleridge, unwilling to challenge comparison with the
divine Bowles, had chosen to describe his sonnets. It
must be honestly said indeed that these are, a very few
excepted, among the least satisfactory productions of
any period of his poetic career. The Coleridgian sonnet
is not only imperfect in form and in marked contrast in
the frequent bathos of its close to the steady swell and
climax of Wordsworth, but, in by far the majority of
instances in this volume, it is wanting in internal weight.
The "single pebble" of thought which a sonnet should
enclose is not only not neatly wrapped up in its envelope
of words, but it is very often not heavy enough to carry
itself and its covering to the mark. When it is so, its
weight, as in the sonnet to Pitt, is too frequently only
another word for an ephemeral violence of political feeling which, whether displayed on one side or the other,
cannot be expected to reproduce its effect in the minds
of comparatively passionless posterity. Extravagances,
too, abound, as when in *Kosciusko* Freedom is made to
look as if, in a fit of "wilfulness and sick despair," she
had drained a mystic urn containing all the tears that
had ever found "fit channel on a Patriot's furrowed
cheek." The main difficulty of the metre, too—that of
avoiding forced rhymes—is rarely surmounted. Even
in the three fine lines in the *Burke*—

" Thee stormy Pity and the cherished lure
Of Pomp and proud precipitance of soul,
Wildered with meteor fires "—

we cannot help feeling that " lure" is extremely harsh,
while the weakness of the two concluding lines of the
sonnet supplies a typical example of the disappointment
which these "effusions" so often prepare for their readers.

Enough, however, has been said of the faults of these
early poems; it remains to consider their merits, foremost
among which, as might be expected, is the wealth and
splendour of their diction in these passages, in which such
display is all that is needed for the literary ends of the
moment. Over all that wide region of literature, in
which force and fervour of utterance, depth and sincerity
of feeling avail, without the nameless magic of poetry in
the higher sense of the word, to achieve the objects of
the writer and to satisfy the mind of the reader, Coleridge
ranges with a free and sure footstep. It is no disparage-
ment to his *Religious Musings* to say that it is to this
class of literature that it belongs. Having said this,
however, it must be added that poetry of the second
order has seldom risen to higher heights of power. The
faults already admitted disfigure it here and there. We
have "moon blasted Madness when he yells at midnight;"
we read of " eye-starting wretches and rapture-trembling
seraphim," and the really striking image of Ruin, the
" old hag, unconquerable, huge, Creation's eyeless
drudge," is marred by making her " nurse" an " impatient earthquake." But there is that in Coleridge's
aspirations and apostrophes to the Deity which im-
presses one even more profoundly than the mere
magnificence, remarkable as it is, of their rhetorical

clothing.   They are touched with so penetrating a
sincerity; they are so obviously the outpourings of an
awe-struck heart.   Indeed, there is nothing more
remarkable at this stage of Coleridge's poetic development than the instant elevation which his verse assumes
whenever he passes to Divine things.   At once it seems
to take on a Miltonic majesty of diction and a Miltonic
stateliness of rhythm.   The tender but low-lying
domestic sentiment of the *Æolian Harp* is in a moment
informed by it with the dignity which marks that poem's
close.   Apart too from its literary merits, the biographical
interest of *Religious Musings* is very considerable.
" Written," as its title declares, but in reality, as its
length would suggest and as Mr. Cottle in fact tells
us, only *completed*, " on the Christmas eve of 1794," it
gives expression to the tumultuous emotions by which
Coleridge's mind was agitated at this its period of
highest political excitement.   His revolutionary enthusiasm was now at its hottest, his belief in the infant
French Republic at its fullest, his wrath against the
" coalesced kings" at its fiercest, his contempt for their
religious pretence at its bitterest.   " Thee to defend," he
cries,

> " Thee to defend, dear Saviour of mankind !
>   Thee, Lamb of God ! Thee, blameless Prince of Peace !
>   From all sides rush the thirsty brood of war—
>   Austria, and that foul Woman of the North,
>   The lustful murderess of her wedded lord,
>   And he, connatural mind ! whom (in their songs,
>   So bards of elder time had haply feigned)
>   Some Fury fondled in her hate to man,
>   Bidding her serpent hair in tortuous fold
>   Lick his young face, and at his mouth imbreathe
>   Horrible sympathy ! "

This is vigorous poetic invective; and the effect of such
outbursts is heightened by the rapid subsidence of the
passion that inspires them and the quick advent of a
calmer mood. We have hardly turned the page ere
denunciations of Catherine and Frederick William give
place to prayerful invocations of the Supreme Being,
which are in their turn the prelude of a long and beautiful contemplative passage : " In the primæval age, a
dateless while," etc., on the pastoral origin of human
society. It is as though some sweet and solemn strain
of organ music had succeeded to the blast of war-bugles
and the roll of drums. In the *Ode to the Departing Year*,
written in the last days of 1796, with its " prophecy of
curses though I pray fervently for blessings " upon the
poet's native country, the mood is more uniform in its
gloom ; and it lacks something, therefore, of those
peculiar qualities which make the *Religious Musings* one
perhaps of the most pleasing of all Coleridge's earlier
productions. But it shares with the poems shortly to
be noticed what may be called the autobiographic charm.
The fresh natural emotion of a young and brilliant mind
is eternally interesting, and Coleridge's youthful Muse,
with a frankness of self-disclosure which is not the less
winning because at times it provokes a smile, confides
to us even the history of her most temporary moods.
It is, for instance, at once amusing and captivating to
read in the latest edition of the poems, as a footnote to
the lines—

> " Not yet enslaved, not wholly vile,
>   O Albion ! O my mother isle ! "

the words—

> " O doomed to fall, enslaved and vile—1796."

Yes ; in 1796 and till the end of 1797 the poet's native
country *was* in his opinion all these dreadful things, but,
directly the mood changes, the verse alters, and to the
advantage, one cannot but think, of the beautiful and
often-quoted close of the passage—

> " And Ocean mid his uproar wild
>   Speaks safety to his island child.
>   Hence for many a fearless age
>   Has social Quiet loved thy shore,
>   Nor ever proud invader's rage,
>   Or sacked thy towers or stained thy fields with gore."

And whether we view him in his earlier or his later
mood there is a certain strange dignity of utterance, a
singular confidence in his own poetic mission, which
forbids us to smile at this prophet of four-and-twenty
who could thus conclude his menacing vaticinations :—

> " Away, my soul, away !
> I, unpartaking of the evil thing,
>   With daily prayer and daily toil
>   Soliciting for food my scanty soil,
>   Have wailed my country with a loud lament.
> Now I recentre my immortal mind
>   In the deep Sabbath of meek self-content,
>   Cleansed from the vaporous passions which bedim
>   God's image, sister of the Seraphim."

If ever the consciousness of great powers and the assurance of a great future inspired a youth with perfect and
on the whole well-warranted fearlessness of ridicule it
has surely done so here.

Poetry alone, however, formed no sufficient outlet for
Coleridge's still fresh political enthusiasm—an enthusiasm
which now became too importunate to let him rest in
his quiet Clevedon cottage.   Was it right, he cries in his

lines of leave-taking to his home, that he should dream away the entrusted hours "while his unnumbered brethren toiled and bled"?   The propaganda of Liberty was to be pushed forward; the principles of Unitarianism, to which Coleridge had become a convert at Cambridge, were to be preached.   Is it too prosaic to add that what poor Henri Murger calls the "chasse aux p;ecès de cent sous" was in all probability demanding peremptorily to be resumed?

Anyhow it so fell out that in the spring of the year 1796 Coleridge took his first singular plunge into the unquiet waters of journalism, instigated thereto by "sundry philanthropists and anti-polemists," whose names he does not record, but among whom we may conjecturally place Mr. Thomas Poole of Stowey, with whom he had formed what was destined to be one of the longest and closest friendships of his life.   Which of the two parties —the advisers or the advised—was responsible for the general plan of this periodical and for the arrangements for its publication is unknown ; but one of these last-mentioned details is enough to indicate that there could have been no "business head" among them.   Considering that the motto of the *Watchman* declared the object of its issue to be that "all might know the truth, and that the truth might make them free," it is to be presumed that the promoters of the scheme were not unwilling to secure as many subscribers as possible for their sheet of "thirty-two pages, large octavo, closely printed, price only fourpence."   In order, however, to exempt it from the stamp-tax, and with the much less practical object of making it "contribute as little as possible to the supposed guilt of a war against freedom," it was to

be published on every eighth day, so that the week-day
of its appearance would of course vary with each successive week—an arrangement as ingeniously calculated
to irritate and alienate its public as any perhaps that
the wit of man could have devised.   So, however, it was
to be, and accordingly with "a flaming prospectus,
'Knowledge is Power,' to cry the state of the political
atmosphere," Coleridge set off on a tour to the north,
from Bristol to Sheffield, for the purpose of procuring
customers, preaching Unitarian sermons by the way in
most of the great towns, "as an hireless volunteer in a
blue coat and white waistcoat that not a rag of the
woman of Babylon might be seen on me."   How he sped
upon his mission is related by him with infinite humour
in the *Biographia Literaria.*   He opened the campaign at
Birmingham upon a Calvinist tallow-chandler, who, after
listening to half an hour's harangue, extending from "the
captivity of the nations" to "the near approach of the
millennium," and winding up with a quotation describ-
ing the latter "glorious state" out of the *Religious Musings,* inquired what might be the cost of the new
publication.   Deeply sensible of "the anti-climax, the
abysmal bathos" of the answer, Coleridge replied,
"Only fourpence, each number to be published every
eighth day," upon which the tallow-chandler observed
doubtfully that that came to "a deal of money at the
end of the year."   What determined him, however, to
withhold his patronage was not the price of the article
but its quantity, and not the deficiency of that quantity
but its excess.   Thirty-two pages, he pointed out, was
more than he ever read all the year round, and though
"as great a one as any man in Brummagem for liberty

and truth, and them sort of things, he begged to be
excused." Had it been possible to arrange for supplying
him with sixteen pages of the paper for twopence, a
bargain might no doubt have been struck; but he
evidently had a business-like repugnance to anything in
the nature of "over-trading." Equally unsuccessful was
a second application made at Manchester to a "stately
and opulent wholesale dealer in cottons," who thrust the
prospectus into his pocket and turned his back upon the
projector, muttering that he was "overrun with these
articles." This, however, was Coleridge's last attempt
at canvassing. His friends at Birmingham persuaded
him to leave that work to others, their advice being no
doubt prompted, in part at least, by the ludicrous
experience of his qualifications as a canvasser which the
following incident furnished them. The same tradesman
who had introduced him to the patriotic tallow-chandler
entertained him at dinner, and, after the meal, invited
his guest to smoke a pipe with him and "two or three
other *illuminati* of the same rank." The invitation was
at first declined on the plea of an engagement to spend
the evening with a minister and his friends, and also
because, writes Coleridge, "I had never smoked except
once or twice in my lifetime, and then it was herb-
tobacco mixed with Oronooko." His host, however,
assured him that the tobacco was equally mild, and
"seeing, too, that it was of a yellow colour," he took
half a pipe of it, "filling the lower half of the bowl," for
some unexplained reason, "with salt." He was soon,
however, compelled to resign it "in consequence of a
giddiness and distressful feeling" in his eyes, which, as
he had drunk but a single glass of ale, he knew must

have been the effect of the tobacco. Deeming himself recovered after a short interval, he sallied forth to fulfil the evening's engagement; but the symptoms returned with the walk and the fresh air, and he had scarcely entered the minister's drawing-room and opened a packet of letters awaiting him there than he "sank back on the sofa in a sort of swoon rather than sleep." Fortunately he had had time to inform his new host of the confused state of his feelings and of its occasion; for "here and thus I lay," he continues, "my face like a wall that is whitewashing, deathly pale, and with the cold drops of perspiration running down it from my forehead; while one after another there dropped in the different gentlemen who had been invited to meet and spend the evening with me, to the number of from fifteen to twenty. As the poison of tobacco acts but for a short time, I at length awoke from insensibility and looked round on the party, my eyes dazzled by the candles, which had been lighted in the interim. By way of relieving my embarrassment one of the gentlemen began the conversation with: 'Have you seen a paper to-day, Mr. Coleridge?' 'Sir,' I replied, rubbing my eyes, 'I am far from convinced that a Christian is permitted to read either newspapers or any other works of merely political and temporary interest.'" The incongruity of this remark, with the purpose for which the speaker was known to have visited Birmingham, and to assist him in which the company had assembled, produced, as was natural, "an involuntary and general burst of laughter," and the party spent, we are told, a most delightful evening. Both then and afterwards, however, they all joined in dissuading the young projector from proceeding with

D

his scheme, assuring him "in the most friendly and yet most flattering expressions" that the employment was neither fit for him nor he for the employment. They insisted that at any rate "he should make no more applications in person, but carry on the canvass by proxy," a stipulation which we may well believe to have been prompted as much by policy as by good nature. The same hospitable reception, the same dissuasion, and, that failing, the same kind exertions on his behalf, he met with at Manchester, Derby, Nottingham, and every other place he visited; and the result of his tour was that he returned with nearly a thousand names on the subscription list of the *Watchman*, together with "something more than a half conviction that prudence dictated the abandonment of the scheme." Nothing but this, however, was needed to induce him to persevere with it. To know that a given course of conduct was the dictate of prudence was a sort of presumptive proof to him at this period of life that the contrary was the dictate of duty. In due time, or rather out of due time,—for the publication of the first number was delayed beyond the day announced for it,—the *Watchman* appeared. Its career was brief—briefer, indeed, than it need have been. A naturally short life was suicidally shortened. In the second number, records Coleridge, with delightful *naïveté*, "an essay against fast-days, with a most censurable application of a text from Isaiah [1] for its motto, lost me near five hundred subscribers at one blow." In the two following numbers he made enemies of all his Jacobin and democratic patrons by playing Balaam to the legislation of the Government, and pronouncing something

[1] "Wherefore my bowels shall sound like an harp."—Is. xvi. 11.

almost like a blessing on the "gagging bills"—measures he declared which, "whatever the motive of their introduction, would produce an effect to be desired by all true friends of freedom, as far as they should contribute to deter men from openly declaiming on subjects the principles of which they had never bottomed, and from pleading to the poor and ignorant instead of pleading for them." At the same time the editor of the *Watchman* avowed his conviction that national education and a concurring spread of the Gospel were the indispensable conditions of any true political amelioration. We can hardly wonder on the whole that by the time the seventh number was published its predecessors were being "exposed in sundry old iron shops at a penny a piece."

And yet, like everything which came from Coleridge's hand, this immature and unpractical production has an interest of its own. Amid the curious mixture of actuality and abstract disquisition of which each number of the *Watchman* is made up, we are arrested again and again by some striking metaphor or some weighty sentence which tells us that the writer is no mere wordy wielder of a facile pen. The paper on the slave trade in the seventh number is a vigorous and, in places, a heart-stirring appeal to the humane emotions. There are passages in it which foreshadow Coleridge's more mature literary manner—the manner of the great pulpit orators of the seventeenth century—in a very interesting way.[1] But what was the use of No. IV. containing

---

[1] Take for instance this sentence : "Our own sorrows, like the Princes of Hell in Milton's Pandemonium, sit enthroned 'bulky and vast ; while the miseries of our fellow-creatures dwindle into pigmy forms, and are crowded in an innumerable multitude into some dark corner of the heart." Both in character of imagery and

an effective article like this when No. III. had opened
with an " Historical Sketch of the Manners and Religion
of the Ancient Germans, introductory to a sketch of the
Manners, Religion, and Politics of present Germany"?
This to a public who wanted to read about Napoleon and
Mr. Pitt! No. III. in all probability "choked off" a good
proportion of the commonplace readers who might have
been well content to have put up with the humanitarian
rhetoric of No. IV., if only for its connection with so unques-
tionable an actuality as West Indian sugar. It was, anyhow, owing to successive alienations of this kind that on
13th May 1796 the editor of the *Watchman* was compelled
to bid farewell to his few remaining readers in the tenth
number of his periodical, for the "short and satisfactory"
reason that " the work does not pay its expenses."
"Part of my readers," continues Coleridge, "relinquished
it because it did not contain sufficient original composition, and a still larger part because it contained too
much ; " and he then proceeds with that half-humorous
simplicity of his to explain what excellent reasons there
were why the first of these classes should transfer their
patronage to Flower's *Cambridge Intelligencer*, and the
second theirs to the *New Monthly Magazine*.

It is not, however, for the biographer or the world to
regret the short career of the *Watchman*, since its
decease left Coleridge's mind in undivided allegiance to

in form of structure we have here the germ of such passages as
this which one might confidently defy the most accomplished
literary "taster" to distinguish from Jeremy Taylor: "Or like
two rapid streams that at their first meeting within narrow and
rocky banks mutually strive to repel each other, and intermix
reluctantly and in tumult, but soon finding a wider channel and
more yielding shores, blend and dilate and flow on in one current
and with one voice."—*Biog. Lit.* p. 155.

the poetic impulse at what was destined to be the period
of its greatest power. In the meantime one result of
the episode had been to make a not unimportant
addition to his friendships. Mention has already been
made of his somewhat earlier acquaintance with Mr.
Thomas Poole of Nether Stowey, a man of high intelligence and mark in his time ; and it was in the course of
his northern peregrinations in search of subscribers that
he met with Charles Lloyd. This young man, the son
of an eminent Birmingham banker, was so struck with
Coleridge's genius and eloquence as to conceive an
" ardent desire to domesticate himself permanently with
a man whose conversation was to him as a revelation
from heaven ; " and shortly after the decease of the
Watchman he obtained his parents' consent to the arrangement.

Early, therefore, in the year 1797 Coleridge, accompanied by Charles Lloyd, removed to Nether Stowey in
Somersetshire, where he occupied a cottage placed at
his disposal by Mr. Poole. His first employment in his
new abode appears to have been the preparation of the
second edition of his poems. In the new issue nineteen
pieces of the former publication were discarded and twelve
new ones added, the most important of which was the
Ode to the Departing Year, which had first appeared in
the *Cambridge Intelligencer*, and had been immediately
afterwards republished in a separate form as a thin
quarto pamphlet, together with some lines of no special
merit " addressed to a young man of fortune " (probably
Charles Lloyd), " who abandoned himself to an indolent
and causeless melancholy." To the new edition were
added the preface already quoted from, and a prose

introduction to the sonnets. The volume also contained
some poems by Charles Lloyd and an enlarged collection
of sonnets and other pieces by Charles Lamb, the latter
of whom about the time of its publication paid his first
visit to the friend with whom, ever since leaving Christ's
Hospital, he had kept up a constant and, to the student
of literature, a most interesting correspondence.[1] In
June 1797 Charles and Mary Lamb arrived at the
Stowey cottage to find their host disabled by an accident
which prevented him from walking during their whole
stay. It was during their absence on a walking expedition that he composed the pleasing lines—

" The lime-tree bower my prison,"

in which he thrice applies to his friend that epithet
which gave such humorous annoyance to the "gentle-
hearted Charles." [2]

But a greater than Lamb, if one may so speak without
offence to the votaries of that rare humorist and exquisite
critic, had already made his appearance on the scene.
Some time before this visit of Lamb's to Stowey Coleridge
had made the acquaintance of the remarkable man who
was destined to influence his literary career in many
ways importantly, and in one way decisively. It was in
the month of June 1797, and at the village of Racedown
in Dorsetshire, that he first met William Wordsworth.

[1] Perhaps a "correspondence" of which only one side exists
may be hardly thought to deserve that name. Lamb's letters
to Coleridge are full of valuable criticism on their respective
poetical efforts. Unfortunately in, it is somewhat strangely said,
"a fit of dejection" he destroyed all Coleridge's letters to him.
[2] Lamb's Correspondence with Coleridge, Letter XXXVII.

CHAPTER III.

Coleridge and Wordsworth — Publication of the *Lyrical
Ballads*—The *Ancient Mariner*—The first part of
Christabel — Decline of Coleridge's poetic impulse—
Final review of his poetry.

[1797-1799.]

THE years 1797 and 1798 are generally and justly
regarded as the blossoming-time of Coleridge's poetic
genius. It would be scarcely an exaggeration to say
that they were even more than this, and that within
the brief period covered by them is included not only
the development of the poet's powers to their full
maturity but the untimely beginnings of their decline.
For to pass from the poems written by Coleridge within
these two years to those of later origin is like passing
from among the green wealth of summer foliage into
the well-nigh naked woods of later autumn. During
1797 and 1798 the *Ancient Mariner*, the first part of
Christabel, the fine ode to France, the *Fears in Solitude*,
the beautiful lines entitled *Frost at Midnight*, the *Nightingale*, the *Circassian Love-Chant*, the piece known as
Love from the poem of the *Dark Ladie*, and that
strange fragment *Kubla Khan*, were all of them written
and nearly all of them published; while between the

last composed of these and that swan-song of his
dying Muse, the *Dejection*, of 1802, there is but one
piece to be added to the list of his greater works.
This therefore, the second part of *Christabel* (1800),
may almost be described by the picturesque image in
the first part of the same poem as

> "The one red leaf, the last of its clan,
>   Hanging so light and hanging so high,
>   On the topmost twig that looks up at the sky."

The first to fail him of his sources of inspiration was
his revolutionary enthusiasm ; and the ode to France—
the *Recantation*, as it was styled on its first appearance in the *Morning Post*—is the record of a reaction
which, as has been said, was as much speedier in Coleridge's case than in that of the other ardent young
minds which had come under the spell of the Revolution as his enthusiasm had been more passionate than
theirs. In the winter of 1797-98 the Directory had
plunged France into an unnatural conflict with her
sister Republic of Switzerland, and Coleridge, who
could pardon and had pardoned her fierce animosity
against a country which he considered not so much his
own as Pitt's, was unable to forgive her this. In the
Recantation he casts her off for ever ; he perceives at last
that true liberty is not to be obtained through political,
but only through spiritual emancipation ; that—

> "The sensual and the dark rebel in vain,
>   Slaves by their own compulsion !   In mad game
>   They burst their manacles, and wear the name
>   Of Freedom graven on a heavier chain";

and arrives in a noble peroration at the somewhat un-
satisfactory conclusion, that the spirit of liberty, "the

guide of homeless winds and playmate of the waves,"
is to be found only among the elements, and not in the
institutions of man.   And in the same quaintly ingenuous spirit which half touches and half amuses us in his
earlier poems he lets us perceive a few weeks later, in
his *Fears in Solitude*, that sympathy with a foreign
nation threatened by the invader may gradually develop
into an almost filial regard for one's own similarly
situated land.   He has been deemed, he says, an enemy
of his country.

> "But, O dear Britain !   O my mother Isle,"

once, it may be remembered, " doomed to fall enslaved
and vile," but now—

> " Needs must thou prove a name most dear and holy,
> To me a son, a brother, and a friend,
> A husband and a father ! who revere
> All bonds of natural love, and find them all
> Within the limits of thy rocky shores."

After all, it has occurred to him, England is not only the
England of Pitt and Grenville, and in that capacity the
fitting prey of the insulted French Republic : she is
also the England of Sara Coleridge, and little Hartley,
and of Mr. Thomas Poole of Nether Stowey.   And so,
to be sure, she was in 1796 when her downfall was
predicted, and in the spirit rather of the Old Testament
than of the New.   But there is something very engaging
in the candour with which the young poet hastens to
apprise us of this his first awakening to the fact.

France may be regarded as the last ode, and *Fears
in Solitude* as the last blank-verse poem of any importance, that owe their origin to Coleridge's early

political sentiments. Henceforth, and for the too brief period of his poetic activity, he was to derive his inspiration from other sources. The most fruitful and important of these was unquestionably his intercourse with Wordsworth, from whom, although there was doubtless a reciprocation of influence between them, his much more receptive nature took a far deeper impression than it made.[1] At the time of their meeting he had already for some three years been acquainted with Wordsworth's works as a poet, and it speaks highly for his discrimination that he was able to discern the great powers of his future friend, even in work so immature in many respects as the *Descriptive Sketches*. It was during the last year of his residence at Cambridge that he first met with these poems, of which he says in the *Biographia Literaria* that "seldom, if ever, was the emergence of an original poetic genius above the literary horizon more evidently announced;" and the effect produced by this volume was steadily enhanced by further acquaintance both with the poet and his works. Nothing, indeed, is so honourably noticeable and even

[1] Perhaps the deepest impress of the Wordsworthian influence is to be found in the little poem *Frost at Midnight*, with its affecting apostrophe to the sleeping infant at his side—infant destined to develop as wayward a genius and to lead as restless and irresolute a life as his father. Its closing lines—

"Therefore all seasons shall be sweet to thee
Whether the summer clothe the general earth
With greenness . . .
. . . whether the eave-drops fall,
Heard only in the trances of the blast,
Or if the secret ministry of frost
Shall hang them up in silent icicles
Quietly shining to the quiet moon"—

might have flowed straight from the pen of Wordsworth himself.

touching in Coleridge's relation to his friend as the tone
of reverence with which, even in the days of his highest
self-confidence and even almost haughty belief in the
greatness of his own poetic mission, he was accustomed
to speak of Wordsworth. A witness, to be more fully
cited hereafter, and whose testimony is especially
valuable as that of one who was by no means blind
to Coleridge's early foible of self-complacency, has
testified to this unbounded admiration of his brother-
poet. "When," records this gentleman, "we have
sometimes spoken complimentarily to Coleridge of
himself he has said that he was nothing in comparison
with Wordsworth." And two years before this, at a
time when they had not yet tested each other's power
in literary collaboration, he had written to Cottle to
inform him of his introduction to the author of "near
twelve hundred lines of blank verse, superior, I dare
aver, to anything in our language which in any way
resembles it," and had declared with evident sincerity
that he felt "a little man" by Wordsworth's side.

His own impression upon his new friend was more
distinctively personal in its origin. It was by Coleridge's
total individuality, by the sum of his vast and varied
intellectual powers, rather than by the specific poetic
element contained in them, that Wordsworth, like the
rest of the world indeed, was in the main attracted;
but it is clear enough that this attraction was from the
first most powerful. On that point we have not only
the weighty testimony of Dorothy Wordsworth, as conveyed in her often-quoted description [1] of her brother's

[1] "You had a great loss in not seeing Coleridge. He is a
wonderful man. His conversation teems with soul, mind, and

new acquaintance, but the still more conclusive evidence
of her brother's own acts. He gave the best possible
proof of the fascination which had been exercised over
him by quitting Racedown with his sister for Alfoxden
near Nether Stowey within a few weeks of his first
introduction to Coleridge, a change of abode for which,
as Miss Wordsworth has expressly recorded, "our
principal inducement was Coleridge's society."

By a curious coincidence the two poets were at this
time simultaneously sickening for what may perhaps
be appropriately called the "poetic measles." They
were each engaged in the composition of a five-act
tragedy, and read scenes to each other, and to each
other's admiration, from their respective dramas. Neither
play was fortunate in its immediate destiny. Wordsworth's tragedy, the *Borderers*, was greatly commended
by London critics and decisively rejected by the management of Covent Garden. As for Coleridge, the negligent
Sheridan did not even condescend to acknowledge the
receipt of his manuscript; his play was passed from hand
to hand among the Drury Lane Committee; but not
till many years afterwards did *Osorio* find its way under
another name to the footlights.

spirit. Then he is so benevolent, so good tempered and cheerful,
and, like William, interests himself so much about every little
trifle. At first I thought him very plain, that is, for about three
minutes ; he is pale, thin, has a wide mouth, thick lips, and not
very good teeth, longish loose-growing half-curling rough black
hair. But if you hear him speak for five minutes you think no
more of them. His eye is large and full, and not very dark but
gray, such an eye as would receive from a heavy soul the dullest
expression ; but it speaks every emotion of his animated mind : it
has more of the poet's eye in a fine frenzy rolling than I ever wit-
nessed. He has fine dark eyebrows and an overhanging forehead."

For the next twelvemonth the intercourse between the two poets was close and constant, and most fruitful in results of high moment to English literature. It was in their daily rambles among the Quantock Hills that they excogitated that twofold theory of the essence and functions of poetry which was to receive such notable illustration in their joint volume of verse, the *Lyrical Ballads ;* it was during a walk over the Quantock Hills that by far the most famous poem of that series, the *Ancient Mariner,* was conceived and in part composed. The publication of the *Lyrical Ballads* in the spring of the year 1798 was, indeed, an event of double significance for English poetry. It marked an epoch in the creative life of Coleridge, and a no less important one in the critical life of Wordsworth. In the *Biographia Literaria* the origination of the plan of the work is thus described :—

" During the first year that Mr. Wordsworth and I were neighbours our conversation turned frequently on the two cardinal points of poetry, the power of exciting the sympathy of the reader by a faithful adherence to the truth of nature, and the power of giving the interest of novelty by the modifying colours of the imagination. The sudden charm which accidents of light and shade, which moonlight or sunset diffused over a known and familiar landscape appeared to represent the practicability of combining both. These are the poetry of nature. The thought suggested itself (to which of us I do not recollect) that a series of poems might be composed of two sorts. In the one the incidents and agents were to be, in part at least, supernatural ; and the interest aimed at was to consist in the interesting of the affections by the dramatic truth of such emotions as would naturally accompany such situations, supposing them real. . . . For the second class, subjects were to be chosen from ordinary life ; the characters and incidents were to be such as will be found in every village and its vicinity where there is a meditative and feeling mind to seek after them, or to notice them when they present themselves. In this idea originated the plan of the *Lyrical Ballads*, in which it was agreed that my endeavours should be directed to persons and characters supernatural, or at least romantic, yet so as to transfer from our inward nature a human interest and a semblance of truth sufficient to procure for these shadows of imagination that willing suspension of disbelief for the moment which constitutes poetic faith. Mr. Wordsworth, on the other hand, was to propose to himself, as his object, to give the charm of novelty to things of everyday, and to excite a feeling analogous to the supernatural by awakening the mind's attention from the lethargy of custom and directing it to the loveliness and the wonders of the world before us; an inexhaustible treasure, but for which, in consequence of the film of familiarity and selfish solicitude, we have eyes which see not, ears that hear not, and hearts which neither feel nor understand."

We may measure the extent to which the poetic teaching and practice of Wordsworth have influenced subsequent taste and criticism by noting how completely the latter of these two functions of poetry has overshadowed the former. To lend the charm of imagination to the real will appear to many people to be not one function of poetry merely but its very essence. To them it *is* poetry, and the only thing worthy of the name; while the correlative function of lending the force of reality to the imaginary will appear at best but a superior kind of metrical romancing, or clever telling of fairy tales. Nor of course can there, from the point of view of the highest conception of the poet's office, be any comparison between the two. In so far as we regard poetry as contributing not merely to the pleasure of the mind but to its health and strength—in so far as we regard it in its capacity not only to delight but to sustain, console, and tranquillise the human spirit—there is, of course, as much difference between the idealistic and the realistic forms of poetry as there is between a narcotic potion and a healing drug. The one, at best, can only enable a man to forget his burdens; the other fortifies him to endure them. It is perhaps no more than was naturally to be expected of our brooding and melancholy age, that poetry (when it is not a mere voluptuous record of the subjective impressions of sense) should have become almost limited in its very meaning to the exposition of the imaginative or spiritual aspect of the world of realities; but so it is now, and so in Coleridge's time it clearly was *not.* Coleridge, in the passage above quoted, shows no signs of regarding one of the two functions which he attributes to poetry as any more accidental or occasional than the other; and the fact that the realistic portion of the *Lyrical Ballads* so far exceeded in amount its supernatural element, he attributes not to any inherent supremacy in the claims of the former to attention but simply to the greater industry which Wordsworth had displayed in his special department of the volume. For his own part, he says, "I wrote the *Ancient Mariner,* and was preparing, among other poems, the *Dark Ladie* and the *Christabel,* in which I should have more nearly realised my ideal than I had done in my first attempt. But Mr. Wordsworth's industry had proved so much more successful, and the number of the poems so much greater, that my compositions, instead of forming a balance, appeared rather an interpolation of heterogeneous matter." There was certainly a considerable disparity between the amount of their respective contributions to the volume, which, in fact, contained nineteen pieces by Wordsworth and only four by Coleridge. Practically, indeed, we may reduce this four to one; for, of the three others, the two scenes from *Osorio* are without special distinction, and the *Nightingale*, though a graceful poem, and containing an admirably-studied description of the bird's note, is too slight and short to claim any importance in the series. But the one long poem which Coleridge contributed to the collection is alone sufficient to associate it for ever with his name. *Unum sed leonem.* To any one who should have taunted him with the comparative infertility of his Muse he might well have returned the haughty answer of the lioness in the fable, when he could point in justification of it to the *Rime of the Ancient Marinere.*

There is, I may assume, no need at the present day to discuss the true place in English literature of this unique product of the human imagination. One is bound, however, to attempt to correlate and adjust it to the rest of the poet's work, and this, it must be admitted, is a most difficult piece of business. Never was there a poem so irritating to a critic of the "pigeon-holing" variety. It simply defies him; and yet the instinct which he obeys is so excusable, because in fact so universal, that one feels guilty of something like disloyalty to the very principles of order in smiling at his disappointment. Complete and symmetrical classification is so fascinating an amusement; it would simplify so many subjects of study, if men and things would only consent to rank themselves under different categories, and remain there; it would, in particular, be so inexpressibly convenient to be able to lay your hand upon your poet whenever you wanted him by merely turning to a shelf

labelled "Realistic" or "Imaginative" (nay, perhaps,
to the still greater saving of labour—Objective or Subjective), that we cannot be surprised at the strength of
the aforesaid instinct in many a critical mind.   Nor
should it be hard to realise its revolt against those single
exceptions which bring its generalisations to nought.
When the pigeon-hole will admit every "document" but
one, the case is hard indeed; and it is not too much to
say that the *Ancient Mariner* is the one document which
the pigeon-hole in this instance declines to admit.   If
Coleridge had only refrained from writing this remarkable poem, or if, having done so, he had written
more poems like it, the critic might have ticketed
him with a quiet mind, and gone on his way com-
placent.   As it is, however, the poet has contrived in
virtue of this performance not only to defeat classification but to defy it.   For the weird ballad abounds in
those very qualities in which Coleridge's poetry with all
its merits is most conspicuously deficient, while on the
other hand it is wholly free from the faults with which
he is most frequently and justly chargeable.   One
would not have said in the first place that the author of
Religious Musings, still less of the *Monody on the Death of
Chatterton*, was by any means the man to have compassed triumphantly at the very first attempt the terse-
ness, vigour, and *naïveté* of the true ballad-manner.
To attain this, Coleridge, the student of his early verse
must feel, would have rather more to retrench and much
more to restrain than might be the case with many other
youthful poets.   The exuberance of immaturity, the
want of measure, the "not knowing where to stop,' are
certainly even more conspicuous in the poems of 1796

than they are in most productions of the same stage of
poetic development; and these qualities, it is needless to
say, require very stern chastening from him who would
succeed in the style which Coleridge attempted for the
first time in the *Ancient Mariner*.

The circumstances of this immortal ballad's birth have
been related with such fulness of detail by Wordsworth,
and Coleridge's own references to them are so completely
reconcilable with that account, that it must have required
all De Quincey's consummate ingenuity as a mischief-
maker to detect any discrepancy between the two.

In the autumn of 1797, records Wordsworth in the
MS. notes which he left behind him, "Mr. Coleridge,
my sister, and myself started from Alfoxden pretty late
in the afternoon with a view to visit Linton and the
Valley of Stones near to it; and as our united funds
were very small, we agreed to defray the expense of the
tour by writing a poem to be sent to the *New Monthly
Magazine*. Accordingly we set off, and proceeded along
the Quantock Hills towards Watchet; and in the course
of this walk was planned the poem of the *Ancient
Mariner*, founded on a dream, as Mr. Coleridge said, of
his friend Mr. Cruikshank. Much the greatest part of
the story was Mr. Coleridge's invention, but certain parts
I suggested; for example, some crime was to be committed which should bring upon the Old Navigator, as
Coleridge afterwards delighted to call him, the spectral
persecution, as a consequence of that crime and his own
wanderings. I had been reading in Shelvocke's *Voyages*,
a day or two before, that while doubling Cape Horn
they frequently saw albatrosses in that latitude, the
largest sort of sea-fowl, some extending their wings

twelve or thirteen feet. 'Suppose,' said I, 'you represent him as having killed one of these birds on entering
the South Sea, and that the tutelary spirits of these
regions take upon them to avenge the crime.' The
incident was thought fit for the purpose, and adopted
accordingly. I also suggested the navigation of the
ship by the dead men, but do not recollect that I had
anything more to do with the scheme of the poem.
The gloss with which it was subsequently accompanied
was not thought of by either of us at the time, at least
not a hint of it was given to me, and I have no doubt it
was a gratuitous afterthought. We began the composition together on that to me memorable evening. I
furnished two or three lines at the beginning of the
poem, in particular—

> 'And listened like a three years' child :
> The Mariner had his will.'

These trifling contributions, all but one, which Mr.
C. has with unnecessary scrupulosity recorded,[1] slipped
out of his mind, as they well might. As we endeavoured to proceed conjointly (I speak of the same
evening) our respective manners proved so widely
different that it would have been quite presumptuous
in me to do anything but separate from an undertaking
upon which I could only have been a clog. . . . The
Ancient Mariner grew and grew till it became too important for our first object, which was limited to our
expectation of five pounds; and we began to think of a

---

[1] The lines—
> "And it is long, and lank, and brown,
> As is the ribbed sea-sand."

volume which was to consist, as Mr. Coleridge has told
the world, of poems chiefly on supernatural subjects."
Except that the volume ultimately determined on was
to consist only "partly" and not "chiefly" of poems on
supernatural subjects (in the result, as has been seen, it
consisted "chiefly" of poems upon natural subjects),
there is nothing in this account which cannot be easily
reconciled with the probable facts upon which De
Quincey bases his hinted charge against Coleridge in
his *Lake Poets*. It was not Coleridge who had been
reading Shelvocke's *Voyages*, but Wordsworth, and it is
quite conceivable, therefore, that the source from which
his friend had derived the idea of the killing of the
albatross may (if indeed he was informed of it at the
time) have escaped his memory twelve years afterwards,
when the conversation with De Quincey took place.
Hence, in "disowning his obligations to Shelvocke," he
may not by any means have intended to suggest that
the albatross incident was his own thought. Moreover,
De Quincey himself supplies another explanation of the
matter, which we know, from the above-quoted notes of
Wordsworth's, to be founded upon fact. "It is possible,"
he adds, "from something which Coleridge said on
another occasion, that before meeting a fable in which
to embody his ideas he had meditated a poem on
delirium, confounding its own dream-scenery with external things, and connected with the imagery of high
latitudes." Nothing, in fact, would be more natural than
that Coleridge, whose idea of the haunted seafarer was
primarily suggested by his friend's dream, and had no
doubt been greatly elaborated in his own imagination
before being communicated to Wordsworth at all, should

have been unable, after a considerable lapse of time, to distinguish between incidents of his own imagining and those suggested to him by others. And, in any case, the "unnecessary scrupulosity," rightly attributed to him by Wordsworth with respect to this very poem, is quite incompatible with any intentional denial of obligations.

Such, then, was the singular and even prosaic origin of the *Ancient Mariner*—a poem written to defray the expenses of a tour; surely the most sublime of "potboilers" to be found in all literature. It is difficult, from amid the astonishing combination of the elements of power, to select that which is the most admirable; but, considering both the character of the story and of its particular vehicle, perhaps the greatest achievement of the poem is the simple realistic force of its narrative. To achieve this was of course Coleridge's main object: he had undertaken to "transfer from our inward nature a human interest and a semblance of truth sufficient to procure for these shadows of imaginations that willing suspension of disbelief for the moment which constitutes poetic faith." But it is easier to undertake this than to perform it, and much easier to perform it in prose than in verse—with the assistance of the everyday and the commonplace than without it. Balzac's *Peau de Chagrin* is no doubt a great feat of the realistic-supernatural; but no one can help feeling how much the author is aided by his "broker's clerk" style of description, and by the familiar Parisian scenes among which he makes his hero move. It is easier to compass verisimilitude in the Palais-Royal than on the South Pacific, to say nothing of the thousand assisting touches, out of place in rhyme

and metre, which can be thrown into a prose narrative.
The *Ancient Mariner*, however, in spite of all these drawbacks, is as real to the reader as is the hero of the *Peau
de Chagrin ;* we are as convinced of the curse upon one of
the doomed wretches as upon the other ; and the strange
phantasmagoric haze which is thrown around the ship
and the lonely voyager leave their outlines as clear as
if we saw them through the sunshine of the streets of
Paris.   Coleridge triumphs over his difficulties by sheer
vividness of imagery and terse vigour of descriptive
phrase—two qualities for which his previous poems did
not prove him to possess by any means so complete a
mastery.   For among all the beauties of his earlier
landscapes we can hardly reckon that of intense and
convincing truth.   He seems seldom before to have
written, as Wordsworth nearly always seems to write,
" with his eye on the object ;" and certainly he never
before displayed any remarkable power of completing
his word-picture with a few touches.   In the *Ancient
Mariner* his eye seems never to wander from his object,
and again and again the scene starts out upon the canvas
in two or three strokes of the brush.   The skeleton
ship, with the dicing demons on its deck ; the setting
sun peering " through its ribs, as if through a dungeon-
grate ; " the water-snakes under the moonbeams, with
the " elfish light " falling off them " in hoary flakes "
when they reared ; the dead crew, who work the ship
and " raise their limbs like lifeless tools "—everything
seems to have been actually *seen*, and we believe it all
as the story of a truthful eye-witness.   The details of
the voyage, too, are all chronicled with such order and
regularity, there is such a diary-like air about the whole

thing, that we accept it almost as if it were a series of
extracts from the ship's "log." Then again the execution—a great thing to be said of so long a poem—is
marvellously equal throughout; the story never drags
or flags for a moment, its felicities of diction are perpetual, and it is scarcely marred by a single weak line.
What could have been better said of the instantaneous
descent of the tropical night than—

> The Sun's rim dips; the stars rush out:
> At one stride comes the dark;"

what more weirdly imagined of the "cracks and
growls" of the rending iceberg than that they sounded
"like noises in a swound"? And how beautifully steals
in the passage that follows upon the cessation of the
spirit's song—

> It ceased; yet still the sails made on
> A pleasant noise till noon,
> A noise like to a hidden brook
> In the leafy month of June,
> That to the sleeping woods all night
> Singeth a quiet tune."

Then, as the ballad draws to its close, after the ship has
drifted over the harbour-bar—

> And I with sobs did pray—
> O let me be awake, my God;
> Or let me sleep alway,"

with what consummate art are we left to imagine the
physical traces which the mariner's long agony had left
behind it by a method far more terrible than any direct
description—the effect, namely, which the sight of him
produces upon others—

> I moved my lips—the Pilot shrieked
> And fell down in a fit;
> The holy Hermit raised his eyes,
> And prayed where he did sit.
>
> I took the oars: the Pilot's boy,
> *Who now doth crazy go,*
> Laughed loud and long, and all the while
> His eyes went to and fro.
> 'Ha! ha!' quoth he, 'full plain I see,
> The Devil knows how to row.'"

Perfect consistency of plan, in short, and complete equality of execution, brevity, self-restraint, and an unerring sense of artistic propriety—these are the chief notes of the *Ancient Mariner*, as they are *not*, in my humble judgment, the chief notes of any poem of Coleridge's before or since. And hence it is that this masterpiece of ballad minstrelsy is, as has been said, so confounding to the "pigeon-holing" mind.

The next most famous poem of this or indeed of any period of Coleridge's life is the fragment of *Christabel*, which, however, in spite of the poet's own opinion on that point, it is difficult to regard as "a more effective realisation" of the "natural-supernatural" idea. Beautiful as it is, it possesses none of that human interest with which, according to this idea, the narrator of the poetic story must undertake to invest it. Nor can the unfinished condition in which it was left be fairly held to account for this, for the characters themselves—the lady Christabel, the witch Geraldine, and even the baron Sir Leoline himself—are somewhat shadowy creations, with too little hold upon life and reality, and too much resemblance to the flitting figures of a dream. Powerful in their way as are the lines descriptive of the

spell thrown over Christabel by her uncanny guest—
lines at the recitation of which Shelley is said to have
fainted—we cannot say that they strike a reader with
such a sense of horror as should be excited by the contemplation of a real flesh-and-blood maiden subdued by
"the shrunken serpent eyes" of a sorceress, and constrained "passively to imitate" their "look of dull and
treacherous hate." Judging it, however, by any other
standard than that of the poet's own erecting, one must
certainly admit the claim of *Christabel* to rank very high
as a work of pure creative art. It is so thoroughly suf-
fused and permeated with the glow of mystical romance,
the whole atmosphere of the poem is so exquisitely
appropriate to the subject, and so marvellously preserved
throughout, that our lack of belief in the reality of the
scenes presented to us detracts but little from the pleasure afforded by the artistic excellence of its present-
ment. It abounds, too, in isolated pictures of surpassing
vividness and grace—word-pictures which live in the
"memory of the eye" with all the wholeness and
tenacity of an actual painting. Geraldine appearing to
Christabel beneath the oak, and the two women stepping
lightly across the hall "that echoes still, pass as lightly
as you will," are pictures of this kind; and nowhere out
of Keats's *Eve of St. Agnes* is there any "interior" to
match that of Christabel's chamber, done as it is in little
more than half a dozen lines. These beauties, it is true,
are fragmentary, like the poem itself, but there is no
reason to believe that the poem itself would have gained
anything in its entirety—that is to say, as a poetic
narrative—by completion. Its main idea—that the
purity of a pure maiden is a charm more powerful for

the protection of those dear to her than the spells of the
evil one for their destruction—had been already sufficiently indicated, and the mode in which Coleridge, it
seems, intended to have worked would hardly have
added anything to its effect.[1] And although he clung
till very late in life to the belief that he *could* have
finished it in after days with no change of poetic
manner—"If easy in my mind," he says in a letter to

[1] Mr. Gillman (in his *Life*, p. 301) gives the following somewhat bald outline of what were to form the two concluding cantos,
no doubt on the authority of Coleridge himself. The second canto
ends, it may be remembered, with the despatch of Bracy the bard
to the castle of Sir Roland :—"Over the mountains the Bard, as
directed by Sir Leoline, hastes with his disciple ; but, in consequence of one of those inundations supposed to be common to the
country, the spot only where the castle once stood is discovered,
the edifice itself being washed away. He determines to return.
Geraldine, being acquainted with all that is passing, like the weird
sisters in *Macbeth*, vanishes. Reappearing, however, she awaits
the return of the Bard, exciting in the meantime by her wily arts
all the anger she could rouse in the Baron's breast, as well as that
jealousy of which he is described to have been susceptible. The
old bard and the youth at length arrive, and therefore she can no
longer personate the character of Geraldine, the daughter of Lord
Roland de Vaux, but changes her appearance to that of the
accepted though absent lover of Christabel. Next ensues a court-
ship most distressing to Christabel, who feels—she knows not why
—great disgust for her once favoured knight. This coldness is
very painful to the Baron, who has no more conception than herself of the supernatural transformation. She at last yields to her
father's entreaties, and consents to approach the altar with the
hated suitor. The real lover returning, enters at this moment,
and produces the ring which she had once given him in sign of
her betrothment. Thus defeated, the supernatural being Geraldine
disappears. As predicted, the castle-bell tolls, the mother's voice
is heard, and, to the exceeding great joy of the parties, the right-
ful marriage takes place, after which follows a reconciliation and
explanation between father and daughter."

be quoted hereafter, "I have no doubt either of the reawakening power or of the kindling inclination "— there are few students of his later poems who will share his confidence. Charles Lamb strongly recommended him to leave it unfinished, and Hartley Coleridge, in every respect as competent a judge on that point as could well be found, always declared his conviction that his father could not, at least *qualis ab incepto*, have finished the poem.

The much-admired little piece first published in the *Lyrical Ballads* under the title of *Love*, and probably best known by its (original) first and most pregnant stanza,[1] possesses a twofold interest for the student of Coleridge's life and works, as illustrating at once one of the most marked characteristics of his peculiar temperament, and one of the most distinctive features of his poetic manner.   The lines are remarkable for a certain strange fascination of melody — a quality for which Coleridge, who was not unreasonably proud of his musical gift, is said to have especially prized them ; and they are noteworthy also as perhaps the fullest expression of the almost womanly softness of Coleridge's nature.   To describe their tone as effeminate would be unfair and untrue, for effeminacy in the work of a male hand would necessarily imply something of falsity of sentiment, and from this they are entirely free.   But it must certainly be admitted that for a man's description of his wooing the warmth of feeling which pervades them is as nearly

---

[1] "All thoughts, all passions, all delights,
  Whatever stirs this mortal frame,
  All are but ministers of Love,
    And feed his sacred flame."

sexless in character as it is possible to conceive; and, beautiful as the verses are, one cannot but feel that they only escape the "namby-pamby" by the breadth of a hair.

As to the wild dream-poem *Kubla Khan*, it is hardly more than a psychological curiosity, and only that perhaps in respect of the completeness of its metrical form. For amid its picturesque but vague imagery there is nothing which might not have presented itself, and the like of which has not perhaps actually presented itself, to many a half-awakened brain of far lower imaginative energy during its hours of full daylight consciousness than that of Coleridge. Nor possibly is it quite an unknown experience to many of us to have even a fully-written record, so to speak, of such impressions imprinted instantaneously on the mind, the conscious composition of whole pages of narrative, descriptive, or cogitative matter being compressed as it were into a moment of time. Unfortunately, however, the impression made upon the ordinary brain is effaced as instantaneously as it is produced; the abnormal exaltation of the creative and apprehensive power is quite momentary, being probably indeed confined to the single moment between sleep and waking; and the mental tablet which a second before was covered so thickly with the transcripts of ideas and images, all far more vivid, or imagined to be so, than those of waking life, and all apprehended with a miraculous simultaneity by the mind, is converted into a *tabula rasa* in the twinkling of a half-opened eye. The wonder in Coleridge's case was that his brain retained the word-impressions sufficiently long to enable him to commit them, to the extent at least of some fifty odd lines, to paper, and that, according to his own belief, this is but a mere fraction of what but for an unlucky interruption in the work of transcribing he would have been able to preserve. His own account of this curious incident is as follows :—

"In the summer of 1797 the author, then in ill health, had retired to a lonely farmhouse between Porlock and Linton, on the Exmoor confines of Somerset and Devonshire. In consequence of a slight indisposition, an anodyne had been prescribed, from the effects of which he fell asleep in his chair at the moment that he was reading, the following sentence, or words of the same substance, in Purchas's *Pilgrimage :*—'Here the Khan Kubla commanded a palace to be built, and a stately garden thereunto. And thus ten miles of fertile ground were enclosed by a wall.' The Author continued for about three hours in a profound sleep, at least of the external senses, during which time he has the most vivid confidence that he could not have composed less than from two to three hundred lines ; if that indeed can be called composition in which all the images rose up before him as things, with a parallel production of the corresponding expressions, without any sensation or consciousness of effort. On awaking he appeared to himself to have a distinct recollection of the whole, and, taking his pen, ink, and paper, instantly and eagerly wrote down the lines that are here preserved. At this moment he was unfortunately called out by a person on business from Porlock, and detained by him above an hour, and on his return to his room found, to his no small surprise and mortification, that though he still retained some vague and dim recollection of the general purport of the vision, yet, with the exception of some eight or ten scattered lines and images, all the rest had passed away like the images on the surface of a stream into which a stone has been cast, but, alas ! without the after restoration of the latter."

This poem, though written in 1797, remained, like *Christabel,* in MS. till 1816. These were then published in a thin quarto volume, together with another piece called the *Pains of Sleep*, a composition of many years' later date than the other two, and of which there will be occasion to say a word or two hereafter.

At no time, however, not even in this the high-tide of its activity, was the purely poetic impulse dominant for long together in Coleridge's mind. He was born with the instincts of the orator, and still more with those of the teacher, and I doubt whether he ever really regarded himself as fulfilling the true mission of his life except at those moments when he was seeking by spoken word to exercise direct influence over his fellow-men. At the same time, however, such was the restlessness of his intellect, and such his instability of purpose, that he could no more remain constant to what he deemed his true vocation than he could to any other. This was now to be signally illustrated. Soon after the *Ancient Mariner* was written, and some time before the volume which was to contain it appeared, Coleridge quitted Stowey for Shrewsbury to undertake the duties of a Unitarian preacher in that town. This was in the month of January 1798,[1] and it seems pretty certain, though exact dates are not to be ascertained, that he was back again at Stowey early in the month of February. In the pages of the *Liberal* (1822) William Hazlitt has given a most graphic and picturesque description of Coleridge's appearance and performance in his Shrews-

---

[1] It may be suggested that this sudden resolution was forced upon Coleridge by the *res angusta domi*. But I do not think that was the case. In the winter of 1797 he had obtained an introduction to and entered into a literary engagement with Mr. Stuart of the *Morning Post*, and could thus have met, as in fact he afterwards did meet, the necessities of the hour.

bury pulpit ; and, judging from this, one can well believe, what indeed was to have been antecedently expected, that had he chosen to remain faithful to his new employment he might have rivalled the reputation of the greatest preacher of the time. But his friends the Wedg-woods, the two sons of the great potter, whose acquaint-ance he had made a few years earlier, were apparently much dismayed at the prospect of his deserting the library for the chapel, and they offered him an annuity of £150 a year on condition of his retiring from the ministry and devoting himself entirely to the study of poetry and philosophy. Coleridge was staying at the house of Hazlitt's father when the letter containing this liberal offer reached him, "and he seemed," says the younger Hazlitt, " to make up his mind to close with the pro-posal in the act of tying on one of his shoes." Another inducement to so speedy an acceptance of it is no doubt to be found in the fact of its presenting to Coleridge an opportunity for the fulfilment of a cherished desire—that, namely, of "completing his education," as he regarded it, by studying the German language, and acquiring an acquaintance with the theology and philo-sophy of Germany in that country itself. This prospect he was enabled, through the generosity of the Wedg-woods, to put into execution towards the end of 1798.

But before passing on from this culminating and, to all intents and purposes, this closing year of Coleridge's career as a poet it will be proper to attempt something like a final review of his poetic work. Admirable as much of that work is, and unique in quality as it is throughout, I must confess that it leaves on my own

mind a stronger impression of the unequal and imperfect
than does that of any poet at all approaching Coleridge
in imaginative vigour and intellectual grasp. It is not
a mere inequality and imperfection of style like that
which so seriously detracts from the pleasure of reading
Byron. Nor is it that the thought is often *impar sibi*
—that, like Wordsworth's, it is too apt to descend from
the mountain-tops of poetry to the flats of commonplace,
if not into the bogs of bathos. In both these respects
Coleridge may and does occasionally offend, but his
workmanship is, on the whole, as much more artistic
than Byron's as the material of his poetry is of more
uniformly equal value than Wordsworth's. Yet, with
almost the sole exception of the *Ancient Mariner*, his
work is in a certain sense more disappointing than that
of either. In spite of his theory as to the twofold
function of poetry we must finally judge that of Coleridge, as of any other poet, by its relation to the actual.
Ancient Mariners and Christabels — the people, the
scenery, and the incidents of an imaginary world—may
be handled by poetry once and again to the wonder and
delight of man ; but feats of this kind cannot—or cannot
in the Western world, at any rate—be repeated indefinitely, and the ultimate test of poetry, at least for the
modern European reader, is its treatment of actualities
—its relations to the world of human action, passion,
sensation, thought. And when we try Coleridge's poetry
in any one of these four regions of life, we seem forced
to admit that, despite all its power and beauty, it at no
moment succeeds in convincing us, as at their best
moments Wordsworth's and even Byron's continually
does, that the poet has found his true poetic vocation—

that he is interpreting that aspect of life which he can interpret better than he can any other, and which no other poet, save the one who has vanquished all poets in their own special fields of achievement, can interpret as well as he. In no poem of actuality does Coleridge so victoriously show himself to be the right man at the right work as does Wordsworth in certain moods of seership and Byron in certain moments of passion. Of them at such moods and moments we feel assured that they have discovered where their real strength lies, and have put it forth to the utmost. But we never feel satisfied that Coleridge has discovered where *his* real strength lies, and he strikes us as feeling no more certainty on the point himself. Strong as is his pinion, his flight seems to resemble rather that of the eaglet than of the full-grown eagle even to the last. He continues "mewing his mighty youth" a little too long. There is a tentativeness of manner which seems to come from a conscious aptitude for many poetic styles and an incapacity to determine which should be definitively adopted and cultivated to perfection. Hence one too often returns from any prolonged ramble through Coleridge's poetry with an unsatisfied feeling which does not trouble us on our return from the best literary country of Byron or Wordsworth. Byron has taken us by rough roads, and Wordsworth led us through some desperately flat and dreary lowlands to his favourite "bits;" but we feel that we have seen mountain and valley, wood and river, glen and waterfall at their best. But Coleridge's poetry leaves too much of the feeling of a walk through a fine country on a misty day. We may have had many a peep of beautiful scenery and occasional glimpses of the

F

sublime ; but the medium of vision has been of variable quality, and somehow we come home with an uneasy suspicion that we have not seen as much as we might.

It is obvious, however, even upon a cursory consideration of the matter, that this disappointing element in Coleridge's poetry is a necessary result of the circumstances of its production ; for the period of his productive activity (at least after attaining manhood) was too short to enable a mind with so many intellectual distractions to ascertain its true poetic bent, and to concentrate its energies thereupon. If he seems always to be feeling his way towards the work which he could do best, it is for the very good reason that this is what, from 1796 to 1800, he was continually doing as a matter of fact. The various styles which he attempted—and for a season, in each case, with such brilliant results— are forms of poetic expression corresponding, on the face of them, to poetic impulses of an essentially fleeting nature. The political or politico-religious odes were the offspring of youthful democratic enthusiasm ; the supernatural poems, so to call them for want of a better name, had their origin in an almost equally youthful and more than equally transitory passion for the wild and wondrous. Political disillusion is fatal to the one impulse, and mere advance in years extinguishes the other. Visions of Ancient Mariners and Christabels do not revisit the mature man, and the Toryism of middle life will hardly inspire odes to anything.

With the extinction of these two forms of creative impulse Coleridge's poetic activity, from causes to be considered hereafter, came almost entirely to an end, and into what later forms it might subsequently have

developed remains therefore a matter more or less of
conjecture.   Yet I think there is almost a sufficiency of
à priori evidence as to what that form would have been.
Had the poet in him survived until years had "brought
the philosophic mind," he would doubtless have done for
the human spirit, in its purely isolated self-communings,
what Wordsworth did for it in its communion with
external nature.   All that the poetry of Wordsworth is
for the mind which loves to hold converse with the
world of things; this, and more perhaps than this—if
more be possible—would the poetry of Coleridge have
been for the mind which abides by preference in the
world of self-originating emotion and introspective
thought.   Wordsworth's primary function is to interpret nature to man: the interpretation of man to himself is with him a secondary process only—the response,
in almost every instance, to impressions from without.
This poet can nobly brace the human heart to fortitude;
but he must first have seen the leech-gatherer on the
lonely moor.   The "presence and the spirit interfused"
throughout creation is revealed to us in moving and
majestic words; yet the poet requires to have felt it "in
the light of setting suns and the round ocean and the
living air" before he feels it "in the mind of man."
But what Wordsworth grants only to the reader who
wanders with him in imagination by lake and mountain,
the Muse of Coleridge, had she lived, would have bestowed upon the man who has entered into his inner
chamber and shut to the door.   This, it seems to me, is
the work for which genius, temperament, and intellectual
habit would alike have fitted him.   For while his feeling
for internal nature was undoubtedly less profound, less

mystically penetrating than Wordsworth's, his sensibilities in general were incomparably quicker and more subtle than those of the friend in whom he so generously recognised a master; and the reach of his sympathies extends to forms of human emotion, to subjects of human interest which lay altogether outside the somewhat narrow range of Wordsworth's.

And, with so magnificent a furniture of those mental and moral qualities which should belong to "a singer of man to men," it must not be forgotten that his technical equipment for the work was of the most splendidly effective kind. If a critic like Mr. Swinburne seems to speak in exaggerated praise of Coleridge's lyrics, we can well understand their enchantment for a master of music like himself. Probably it was the same feeling which made Shelley describe *France* as "the finest ode in the English language." With all, in fact, who hold—as it is surely plausible to hold—that the first duty of a singer is to sing, the poetry of Coleridge will always be more likely to be classed above than below its merits, great as they are. For, if we except some occasional lapses in his sonnets—a metrical form in which, at his best, he is quite "out of the running" with Wordsworth—his melody never fails him. He is a singer always, as Wordsworth is not always, and Byron almost never. The Æolian harp to which he so loved to listen does not more surely respond in music to the breeze of heaven than does Coleridge's poetic utterance to the wind of his inspiration. Of the dreamy fascination which *Love* exercises over a listening ear I have already spoken; and there is hardly less charm in the measure and assonances of the *Circassian Love Chant*. *Christabel* again, considered

solely from the metrical point of view, is a veritable
tour de force—the very model of a metre for romantic
legend : as which, indeed, it was imitated with sufficient
grace and spirit, but seldom with anything approaching
to Coleridge's melody, by Sir Walter Scott.

Endowed therefore with so glorious a gift of song,
and only not fully master of his poetic means because of
the very versatility of his artistic power and the very
variety and catholicity of his youthful sympathies, it is
unhappily but too certain that the world has lost much
by that perversity of conspiring accidents which so untimely silenced Coleridge's muse.   And the loss is the
more trying to posterity because he seems, to a not, I
think, too curiously considering criticism, to have once
actually struck that very chord which would have
sounded the most movingly beneath his touch,—and to
have struck it at the very moment when the failing hand
was about to quit the keys for ever.

> " Ostendunt terris hunc tantum fata neque ultra
> Esse sinunt."

I cannot regard it as merely fantastic to believe that
the *Dejection*, that dirge of infinite pathos over the grave
of creative imagination, might, but for the fatal decree
which had by that time gone forth against Coleridge's
health and happiness, have been but the cradle-cry of
a new-born poetic power, in which imagination, not an-
nihilated but transmigrant, would have splendidly proved
its vitality through other forms of song.

CHAPTER IV

Visit to Germany—Life at Göttingen—Return—Explores
the Lake Country—London—The *Morning Post*—Coleridge as a journalist—Retirement to Keswick.

[1799-1800.]

THE departure of the two poets for the Continent was
delayed only till they had seen their joint volume
through the press. The *Lyrical Ballads* appeared in
the autumn of 1798, and on 16th September of that
year Coleridge left Yarmouth for Hamburg with
Wordsworth and his sister.[1] The purpose of his two
companions' tour is not known to have been other than
the pleasure, or mixed pleasure and instruction, usually
derivable from foreign travel; that of Coleridge was
strictly, even sternly, educational. Immediately on
his arrival in Germany he parted from the Wordsworths,

---

[1] De Quincey's error, in supposing that Coleridge's visit to
Germany to " complete his education " was made at an earlier date
than this journey with the Wordsworths, is a somewhat singular
mistake for one so well acquainted with the facts of Coleridge's
life. Had we not his own statement that this of 1798 was the
first occasion of his quitting his native country, it so happens that
we can account in England for nearly every month of his time
from his leaving Cambridge until this date.

who went on to Gozlar,[1] and took up his abode at the
house of the pastor at Ratzeburg, with whom he spent
five months in assiduous study of the language. In
January he removed to Göttingen. Of his life here
during the next few months we possess an interesting
record in the *Early Years and Late Reflections* of
Dr. Carrlyon, a book published many years after the
events which it relates, but which is quite obviously a
true reflection of impressions yet fresh in the mind of
its writer when its materials were first collected. Its
principal value, in fact, is that it gives us Coleridge
from the standpoint of the average young educated
Englishman of the day, sufficiently intelligent, indeed,
to be sensible of his fellow-student's transcendent
abilities, but as little awed by them out of youth's
healthy irreverence of criticism as the ordinary English undergraduate ever has been by the intellectual
supremacy of any "greatest man of his day" who
might chance to have been his contemporary at Oxford
or Cambridge. In Dr. Carrlyon's reminiscences and in
the quoted letters of a certain young Parry, another
of the English student colony at Göttingen, we get a
piquant picture of the poet-philosopher of seven-and-
twenty, with his yet buoyant belief in his future, his
still unquenched interest in the world of things, and his

[1] It has only within a comparatively recent period been
ascertained that the visit of the Wordsworths to Germany was
itself another result of Thomas Wedgwood's generous appreciation
of literary merit. It appears, on the incontrovertible testimony of
the Wedgwoods' accounts with their agents at Hamburg, that the
expenses of all three travellers were defrayed by their friend at
home. The credits opened for them amounted, during the course
of their stay abroad, to some £260.—Miss Meteyard's *A Group of
Englishmen*, p. 99.

never-to-be-quenched interest in the world of thought,
his even then inexhaustible flow of disquisition, his
generous admiration for the gifts of others, and his
naïve complacency—including, it would seem, a touch of
the vanity of personal appearance—in his own.   "He
frequently," writes Dr. Carrlyon, "recited his own
poetry, and not unfrequently led us further into the
labyrinth of his metaphysical elucidations, either of
particular passages or of the original conception of any
of his productions, than we were able to follow him.
At the conclusion, for instance, of the first stanza of
Christabel, he would perhaps comment at full length
upon such a line as 'Tu—whit !——Tu—whoo !' that we
might not fall into the mistake of supposing originality
to be its sole merit."   The example is not very happily
chosen, for Coleridge could hardly have claimed "originality" for an onomatopœia which occurs in one of
Shakspeare's best known lyrics; but it serves well
enough to illustrate the fact that he "very seldom went
right to the end of any piece of poetry ; to pause and
analyse was his delight."   His disappointment with
regard to his tragedy of *Osorio* was, we also learn, still
fresh.   He seldom, we are told, "recited any of the
beautiful passages with which it abounds without a
visible interruption of the perfect composure of his
mind."   He mentioned with great emotion Sheridan's
inexcusable treatment of him with respect to it.   At
the same time, adds his friend, "he is a severe critic of
his own productions, and declares" (this no doubt with
reference to his then, and indeed his constant estimate
of *Christabel* as his masterpiece) "that his best poems
have perhaps not appeared in print."

Young Parry's account of his fellow-student is also
fresh and pleasing. "It is very delightful," he tells a
correspondent, "to hear him sometimes discourse on
religious topics for an hour together. His fervour is
particularly agreeable when compared with the chilling
speculations of German philosophers," whom Coleridge,
he adds, "successively forced to abandon all their
strongholds." He is "much liked, notwithstanding many
peculiarities. He is very liberal towards all doctrines
and opinions, and cannot be put out of temper. These
circumstances give him the advantage of his opponents,
who are always bigoted and often irascible. Coleridge
is an enthusiast on many subjects, and must therefore
appear to many to possess faults, and no doubt he has
faults, but he has a good heart and a large mass of
information with," as his fellow-student condescendingly
admits, "superior talents. The great fault which his
friends may lament is the variety of subjects which he
adopts, and the abstruse nature of his ordinary speculations, *extra homines positas.* They can easily," concludes
the writer, rising here to the full stateliness of youth's
epistolary style, "they can easily excuse his devoted
attachment to his country, and his reasoning as to the
means of producing the greatest human happiness, but
they do not universally approve the mysticism of his
metaphysics and the remoteness of his topics from
human comprehension."

In the month of May 1799 Coleridge set out with a
party of his fellow-students on a walking tour through
the Harz Mountains, an excursion productive of much
oral philosophising on his part, and of the composition
of the *Lines on ascending the Brocken,* not one of the

happiest efforts of his muse. As to the philosophising, "he never," says one of his companions on this trip, "appeared to tire of mental exercise; talk seemed to him a perennial pastime, and his endeavours to inform and amuse us ended only with the cravings of hunger or the fatigue of a long march, from which neither his conversational powers nor his stoicism could protect himself or us." It speaks highly for the matter of Coleridge's allocutions that such incessant outpourings during a mountaineering tramp appear to have left no lasting impression of boredom behind them. The holiday seems to have been thoroughly enjoyed by the whole party, and Coleridge, at any rate, had certainly earned it. For once, and it is almost to be feared for the last time in his life, he had resisted his besetting tendency to dispersiveness, and constrained his intelligence to apply itself to one thing at a time. He had come to Germany to acquire the language, and to learn what of German theology and metaphysics he might find worth the study, and his five months' steady pursuit of the former object had been followed by another four months of resolute prosecution of the latter. He attended the lectures of Professor Blumenbach, and obtained through a fellow-student notes from those of Eichhorn. He suffered no interruption in his studies, unless we are to except a short visit from Wordsworth and his sister, who had spent most of their stay abroad in residence at Gozlar; and he appears, in short, to have made in every way the best use of his time. On 24th June 1799 he gave his leave-taking supper at Gottingen, replying to the toast of his health in fluent German but with an execrable accent; and the next day presumably he started on his homeward journey.

His movements for the next few months are incorrectly stated in most of the brief memoirs prefixed to the various editions of the poet's works,—their writers having, it is to be imagined, accepted without examination a misplaced date of Mr. Gillman's. It is not the fact that Coleridge "returned to England after an absence of fourteen months, and arrived in London the 27th of November." His absence could not have lasted longer than a year, for we know from the evidence of Miss Wordsworth's diary that he was exploring the Lake country (very likely for the first time) in company with her brother and herself in the month of September 1799. The probability is that he arrived in England early in July, and immediately thereupon did the most natural and proper thing to be done under the circumstances—namely, returned to his wife and children at Nether Stowey, and remained there for the next two months, after which he set off with the Wordsworths, then still at Alfoxden, to visit the district to which the latter had either already resolved upon, or were then contemplating, the transfer of their abode.

The 27th of November is no doubt the correct date of his arrival in London, though not "from abroad." And his first six weeks in the metropolis were spent in a very characteristic fashion—in the preparation, namely, of a work which he pronounced with perfect accuracy to be destined to fall dead from the press. He shut himself up in a lodging in Buckingham Street, Strand, and by the end of the above-mentioned period he had completed his admirable translation of *Wallenstein*, in itself a perfect, and indeed his most perfect dramatic poem. The manuscript of this English version of Schiller's drama was purchased by Messrs. Longman under the condition that the translation and the original should appear at the same time. Very few copies were sold, and the publishers, indifferent to Coleridge's advice to retain the unsold copies until the book should become fashionable, disposed of them as waste paper. Sixteen years afterwards, on the publication of *Christabel*, they were eagerly sought for, and the few remaining copies doubled their price. It was while engaged upon this work that he formed that connection with political journalism which lasted, though with intermissions, throughout most of the remainder of his life. His early poetical pieces had, as we have seen, made their first appearance in the *Morning Post*, but hitherto that newspaper had received no prose contribution from his pen. His engagement with its proprietor, Mr. Daniel Stuart, to whom he had been introduced during a visit to London in 1797, was to contribute an occasional copy of verses for a stipulated annual sum; and some dozen or so of his poems (notably among them the ode to *France* and the two strange pieces *Fire Famine and Slaughter* and *The Devil's Thoughts*) had entered the world in this way during the years 1798 and 1799.

Misled by the error above corrected, the writers of some of the brief memoirs of Coleridge's life represent him as having sent verse contributions to the *Morning Post* from Germany in 1799; but as the earliest of these only appeared in August of that year there is no reason to suppose that any of them were written before his return to England. The longest of the serious pieces is the well-known *Ode to Georgiana, Duchess of Devon-shire,* which cannot be regarded as one of the happiest of Coleridge's productions. Its motive is certainly a little slight, and its sentiment more than a little over-strained. The noble enthusiasm of the noble lady who, "though nursed in pomp and pleasure," could yet con-descend to "hail the platform wild where once the Austrian fell beneath the shaft of Tell," hardly strikes a reader of the present day as remarkable enough to be worth "gushing" over; and when the poet goes on to suggest as the explanation of Georgiana's having "learned that heroic measure" that the Whig great lady had suckled her own children, we certainly seem to have taken the fatal step beyond the sublime ! It is to be presumed that Tory great ladies invariably employed the services of a wet-nurse, and hence failed to win the same tribute from the angel of the earth, who, usually, while he guides

> "His chariot-planet round the goal of day,
> All trembling gazes on the eye of God,"

but who on this occasion "a moment turned his awful face away " to gaze approvingly on the high-born mother who had so conscientiously performed her maternal duties.

Very different is the tone of this poem from that of the two best known of Coleridge's lighter contributions to the *Morning Post.* The most successful of these, however, from the journalistic point of view, is in a literary sense the less remarkable. One is indeed a little astonished to find that a public, accustomed to such admirable political satire as the *Anti-Jacobin,* should have been so much taken as it seems to have been by the rough versification and somewhat clumsy sarcasm of the *Devil's Thoughts*. The poem created something like a *furore*, and sold a large reissue of the number of the *Morning Post* in which it appeared. Nevertheless it is from the metrical point of view doggerel, as indeed the author admits, three of its most smoothly-flowing stanzas being from the hand of Southey, while there is nothing in its boisterous political drollery to put its composition beyond the reach of any man of strong partisan feelings and a turn for street-humour. *Fire Famine and Slaughter*, on the other hand, is literary in every sense of the word, requiring indeed, and very urgently, to insist on its character as literature, in order to justify itself against the charge of inhuman malignity. Despite the fact that "letters four do form his name," it is of course an idealised statesman, and not the real flesh and blood Mr. Pitt, whom the sister furies, Fire, Famine, and Slaughter, extol as their patron in these terrible lines. The poem must be treated as what lawyers call an "A. B. case." Coleridge must be supposed to be lashing certain alphabetical symbols arranged in a certain order. This idealising process is perfectly easy and familiar to everybody with the literary sense. The deduction for " poetic license " is just as readily, though it does not, of course, require to be as frequently, made with respect to the hyperbole of denunciation as with respect to that of praise. Nor need we doubt that this deduction had in fact been made by all intelligent readers long before that agitating dinner at Mr. Sotheby's, which Coleridge describes with such anxious gravity in his apologetic preface to the republication of the lines. On the whole one may pretty safely accept De Quincey's

view of the true character of this incident as related by
him in his own inimitable fashion, namely, that it was
in the nature of an elaborate hoax, played off at the
poet's expense.[1]   The malice of the piece is, as De
Quincey puts it, quite obviously a "malice of the understanding and fancy," and not of the heart.   There
is significance in the mere fact that the poem was
deliberately published by Coleridge two years after its
composition, when the vehemence of his political ani-
mosities had much abated.   Written in 1796, it did not
appear in the *Morning Post* till January 1798.

He was now, however, about to draw closer his connection with the newspaper press.   Soon after his
return from Germany he was solicited to "undertake
the literary and political department in the *Morning Post*,"

---

[1] After quoting the two concluding lines of the poem, "Fire's"
rebuke of her inconstant sisters, in the words

"I alone am faithful, I
Cling to him everlastingly,"

De Quincey proceeds : "The sentiment is diabolical ; and the
question argued at the London dinner-table (Mr. Sotheby's) was
'Could the writer have been other than a devil ?' . . . Several of the
great guns among the literary body were present—in particular
Sir Walter Scott, and he, we believe, with his usual good nature,
took the apologetic side of the dispute ; in fact, he was in the
secret.   Nobody else, barring the author, knew at first whose good
name was at stake.   The scene must have been high.   The company kicked about the poor diabolic writer's head as though it had
been a tennis-ball.   Coleridge, the yet unknown criminal, absolutely
perspired and fumed in pleading for the defendant ; the company
demurred ; the orator grew urgent ; wits began to *smoke* the case
as an active verb, the advocate to smoke as a neuter verb ; the
'fun grew fast and furious,' until at length the delinquent arose,
burning tears in his eyes, and confessed to an audience now bursting with stifled laughter (but whom he supposed to be bursting
with fiery indignation), 'Lo, I am he that wrote it.'"

and acceded to the proposal "on condition that the paper should thenceforward be conducted on certain fixed and announced principles, and that he should be neither obliged nor requested to deviate from them in favour of any party or any event." Accordingly, from December 1799 until about midsummer of 1800, Coleridge became a regular contributor of political articles to this journal, sometimes to the number of two or three in one week. At the end of the period of six months he quitted London, and his contributions became necessarily less frequent, but they were continued (though with two apparent breaks of many months in duration)[1] until the close of the year 1802. It would seem, however, that nothing but Coleridge's own disinclination prevented this connection from taking a form in which it would have profoundly modified his whole future career. In a letter to Mr. Poole, dated March 1800, he informs his friend that if he "had the least love of money" he could "make sure of £2000 a year, for that Stuart had offered him half shares in his two papers, the *Morning Post* and the *Courier*, if he would devote himself to them in conjunction with their proprietor. But I told him," he continues, "that I would not give up the country and the lazy reading of old folios for two thousand times two thousand pounds,—in short, that beyond £350 a year I considered money as a real evil." Startlingly liberal as

---

[1] *Sic* in *Essays on his own Times* by S. T. C., the collection of her father's articles made by Mrs. Nelson (Sara) Coleridge ; but without attributing strange error to Coleridge's own estimate (in the *Biographia Literaria*) of the amount of his journalistic work, it is impossible to believe that this collection, forming as it does but two small volumes, and a portion of a third, is anything like complete.

this offer will appear to the journalist, it seems really to have been made. For, writing long afterwards to Mr. Nelson Coleridge, Mr. Stuart says: "Could Coleridge and I place ourselves thirty years back, and he be so far a man of business as to write three or four hours a day, there is nothing I would not pay for his assistance. I would take him into partnership, and I would enable him to make a large fortune." Nor is there any reason to think that the bargain would have been a bad one for the proprietor from the strictly commercial point of view. Coleridge in later years may no doubt have over-rated the effect of his own contributions on the circula-tion of the *Morning Post*, but it must have been beyond question considerable, and would in all likelihood have become far greater if he could have been induced to devote himself more closely to the work of journalism. For the fact is—and it is a fact for which the current con-ception of Coleridge's intellectual character does not altogether prepare one—that he was a workman of the very first order of excellence in this curious craft. The faculties which go to the attainment of such excellence are not perhaps among the highest distinctions of the human mind, but, such as they are, they are specific and well marked; they are by no means the necessary accom-paniments even of the most conspicuous literary power, and they are likely rather to suffer than to profit by association with great subtlety of intellect or wide philosophic grasp. It is not to the advantage of the journalist, as such, that he should see too many things at a time, or too far into any one thing, and even the gifts of an active imagination and an abundant vocabulary are each of them likely to prove a snare. To be wholly

successful, the journalist—at least the English journalist—
must not be too eloquent, or too witty, or too humorous,
or too ingenious, or too profound. Yet the English
reader likes, or thinks he likes, eloquence; he has a keen
sense of humour, and a fair appreciation of wit ; and he
would be much hurt if he were told that ingenuity and
profundity were in themselves distasteful to him. How,
then, to give him enough of these qualities to please and
not enough to offend him—as much eloquence as will
stir his emotions, but not enough to arouse his distrust;
as much wit as will carry home the argument, but not
enough to make him doubt its sincerity; as much humour
as will escape the charge of levity, as much ingenuity as
can be displayed without incurring suspicion, and as
much profundity as may impress without bewildering ?
This is a problem which is fortunately simplified for
most journalists by the fact of their possessing these
qualities in no more than, if in so much as, the minimum
required.   But Coleridge, it must be remembered, possessed most of them in embarrassing superfluity. Not
all of them indeed, for, though he could be witty and at
times humorous, his temptations to excess in these
respects were doubtless not considerable. But as for his
eloquence, he was from his youth upwards *Isæo torrentior*,
his dialectical ingenuity was unequalled, and in disquisition of the speculative order no man was so apt as he
to penetrate more deeply into his subject than most of
his readers would care to follow him. . *A priori*, therefore, one would have expected that Coleridge's instincts
would have led him to rhetorise too much in his diction,
to refine too much in his arguments, and to philosophise
too much in his reflections, to have hit the popular

taste as a journalist, and that at the age of eight-and-twenty he would have been unable to subject these tendencies either to the artistic repression of the maturer writer or to the tactical restraints of the trained advocate. This eminently natural assumption, however, is entirely rebutted by the facts. Nothing is more remarkable in Coleridge's contributions to the *Morning Post* than their thoroughly workmanlike character from the journalistic point of view, their avoidance of "viewiness," their strict adherence to the one or two simple points which he is endeavouring at any particular juncture in politics to enforce upon his readers, and the steadiness with which he keeps his own and his readers' attention fixed on the special political necessities of the hour. His articles, in short, belong to that valuable class to which, while it gives pleasure to the cultivated reader, the most commonplace and Philistine man of business cannot refuse the to him supreme praise of being eminently "practical." They hit the nail on the head in nearly every case, and they take the plainest and most direct route to their point, dealing in rhetoric and metaphor only so far as the strictly "business" ends of the argument appear to require. Nothing, for instance, could have been better done, better reasoned and written, more skilfully adapted throughout to the English taste, than Coleridge's criticism (31st Dec. 1799) on the new constitution established by Bonaparte and Sieyes on the foundation of the Consulate, with its eighty senators, the "creatures of a renegade priest, himself the creature of a foreign mercenary, its hundred tribunes who are to talk and do nothing, and its three hundred legislators whom the constitution orders to be silent." What a ludicrous

Purgatory, adds he, " for three hundred Frenchmen ! "
Very vigorous, moreover, is he on the ministerial rejection of the French proposals of peace in 1800, arguing
against the continuance of the war on the very sound
anti-Jacobin ground that if it were unsuccessful it would
inflame French ambition anew, and, if successful, repeat
the experience of the results of rendering France
desperate, and simply reanimate Jacobinism.

Effective enough too, for the controversial needs of
the moment, was the argument that if France were
known, as Ministers pretended, to be insincere in
soliciting peace; "Ministers would certainly treat with
her, since they would again secure the support of the
British people in the war, and expose the ambition of
the enemy ; " and that, therefore, the probability was
that the British Government knew France to be sincere,
and shrank from negotiation lest it should expose their
own desire to prosecute the war.[1]   Most happy, again,
is his criticism of Lord Grenville's note, with its references to the unprovoked aggression of France (in the
matter of the opening of the Scheldt, etc.) as the sole
cause and origin of the war.   "If this were indeed true,
in what ignorance must not Mr. Pitt and Mr. Windham
have kept the poor Duke of Portland, who declared in
the House of Lords that the cause of the war was the
maintenance of the Christian religion ? "

To add literary excellence of the higher order to the

---

[1] Alas, that the facts should be so merciless to the most excellent arguments ! Coleridge could not foresee that.Napoleon would,
years afterwards, admit in his own Memoirs the insincerity of his
overtures.   "I had need of war ; a treaty of peace . . . would
have withered every imagination."   And when Mr. Pitt's answer
arrived, "it filled me with a secret satisfaction."

peculiar qualities which give force to the newspaper
article is for a journalist, of course, a "counsel of perfection;" but it remains to be remarked that Coleridge did
make this addition in a most conspicuous manner.
Mrs. H. N. Coleridge's three volumes of her father's
Essays on his own Times deserve to live as literature
apart altogether from their merits as journalism. Indeed
among the articles in the *Morning Post* between 1799
and 1802 may be found some of the finest specimens of
Coleridge's maturer prose style. The character of Pitt,
which appeared on 19th March 1800, is as remarkable for
its literary merits as it is for the almost humorous
political perversity which would not allow the Minister
any single merit except that which he owed to the
sedulous rhetorical training received by him from his
father, viz. "a premature and unnatural dexterity in the
combination of words."[1] The letters to Fox, again,
though a little artificialised perhaps by reminiscences of
Junius, are full of weight and dignity. But by far the
most piquant illustration of Coleridge's peculiar power is
to be found in the comparison between his own version
of Pitt's speech of 17th February 1800, on the continuance

---

[1] The following passage, too, is curious as showing how polemics,
like history, repeat themselves. "As his reasonings were, so is his
eloquence. One character pervades his whole being. Words on
words, finely arranged, and so dexterously consequent that the
whole bears the semblance of argument and still keeps awake a
sense of surprise; but, when all is done, nothing rememberable has
been said; no one philosophical remark, no one image, not even a
pointed aphorism. Not a sentence of Mr. Pitt's has ever been
quoted, or formed the favourite phrase of the day—a thing un-
exampled in any man of equal reputation." With the alteration of
one word—the proper name—this passage might have been taken
straight from some political diatribe of to-day.

of the war, with the report of it which appeared in the
Times of that date.   With the exception of a few
unwarranted elaborations of the arguments here and
there, the two speeches are in substance identical; but
the effect of the contrast between the minister's cold
state-paper periods and the life and glow of the poet-
journalist's style is almost comic.   Mr. Gillman records
that Canning, calling on business at the editor's, inquired, as others had done, who was the reporter of
the speech for the *Morning Post*, and, on being told,
remarked drily that the report "did more credit to his
head than to his memory."

On the whole one can well understand Mr. Stuart's
anxiety to secure Coleridge's permanent collaboration
with him in the business of journalism; and it would be
possible to maintain, with less of paradox than may at
first sight appear, that it would have been better not
only for Coleridge himself but for the world at large if
the editor's efforts had been successful.   It would indeed
have been bowing the neck to the yoke; but there are
some natures upon which constraint of that sort exercises
not a depressing but a steadying influence.   What, after
all, would the loss in hours devoted to a comparatively
inferior class of literary labour have amounted to when
compared with the gain in much-needed habits of method
and regularity, and—more valuable than all to an intellect
like Coleridge's,—in the constant reminder that human
life is finite and the materials of human speculation
infinite, and that even a world-embracing mind must
apportion its labour to its day?   There is, however, the
great question of health to be considered—*the* question, as
every one knows, of Coleridge's whole career and life.   If

health was destined to give way, in any event—if its
collapse, in fact, was simply the cause of all the lamentable
external results which followed it, while itself due only
to predetermined internal conditions over which the
sufferer had no control—then to be sure *cadit quæstio.*
At London or at the Lakes, among newspaper files or
old folios, Coleridge's life would in that case have run
the same sad course; and his rejection of Mr. Stuart's
offer becomes a matter of no particular interest to disappointed posterity.   But be that as it may, the "old
folios" won the day.   In the summer of 1800 Coleridge
quitted London, and having wound up his affairs at his
then place of residence, removed with his wife and children to a new and beautiful home in that English Lake
country with which his name was destined, like those of
Southey and Wordsworth, to be enduringly associated.

CHAPTER V.

Life at Keswick—Second part of *Christabel*—Failing health —Resort to opium—The *Ode to Dejection*—Increasing restlessness—Visit to Malta.

[1800-1804.]

WE are now approaching the turning-point, moral and physical, of Coleridge's career. The next few years determined not only his destiny as a writer but his life as a man. Between his arrival at Keswick in the summer of 1800 and his departure for Malta in the spring of 1804 that fatal change of constitution, temperament, and habits which governed the whole of his subsequent history had fully established itself. Between these two dates he was transformed from the Coleridge of whom his young fellow-students in Germany have left us so pleasing a picture into the Coleridge whom distressed kinsmen, alienated friends, and a disappointed public were to have before them for the remainder of his days. Here, then, at Keswick, and in these first two or three years of the century—here or nowhere is the key to the melancholy mystery to be found.

It is probable that only those who have gone with some minuteness into the facts of this singular life are

aware how great was the change effected during this
very short period of time. When Coleridge left London
for the Lake country he had not completed his eight-and-
twentieth year. Before he was thirty he wrote that
Ode to Dejection in which his spiritual and moral losses
are so pathetically bewailed. His health and spirits, his
will and habits, may not have taken any unalterable
bent for the worse until 1804, the year of his departure
for Malta—the date which I have thought it safest to
assign as the definitive close of the earlier and happier
period of his life; but undoubtedly the change had fully
manifested itself more than two years before. And a
very great and painful one it assuredly was. We know
from the recorded evidence of Dr. Carrlyon and others
that Coleridge was full of hope and gaiety, full of confidence in himself and of interest in life during his few
months' residence in Germany. The *annus mirabilis*
of his poetic life was but two years behind him, and his
achievements of 1797-98 seemed to him but a mere earnest
of what he was destined to accomplish. His powers of
mental concentration were undiminished, as his student
days at Göttingen sufficiently proved; his conjugal and
family affections, as Dr. Carrlyon notes for us, were still
unimpaired; his own verse gives signs of a home-sickness
and a yearning for his own fireside which were in
melancholy contrast with the restlessness of his later
years. Nay, even after his return to England, and
during the six months of his regular work on the *Morning
Post*, the vigour of his political articles entirely negatives
the idea that any relaxation of intellectual energy had as
yet set in. Yet within six months of his leaving London
for Keswick there begins a progressive decline in Cole-

ridge's literary activity in every form. The second part of *Christabel*, beautiful but inferior to the first, was composed in the autumn of 1800, and for the next two years, so far as the higher forms of literature are concerned, "the rest is silence." The author of the prefatory memoir in the edition of Coleridge's *Poetical and Dramatic Works* (1880), enumerates some half-dozen slight pieces contributed to the *Morning Post* in 1801, but declares that Coleridge's poetical contributions to this paper during 1802 were "very rich and varied, and included the magnificent ode entitled *Dejection*." Only the latter clause of this statement is entitled, I think, to command our assent. Varied though the list may be, it is hardly to be described as "rich." It covers only about seven weeks in the autumn of 1802, and, with the exception of the *Lovers' Resolution* and the "magnificent ode" referred to, the pieces are of the shortest and slightest kind. Nor is it accurate to say that the "political articles of the same period were also numerous and important." On the contrary, it would appear from an examination of Mrs. H. N. Coleridge's collection that her father's contributions to the *Post* between his departure from London and the autumn of 1802 were few and intermittent, and in August 1803 the proprietorship of that journal passed out of Mr. Stuart's hands. It is, in short, I think, impossible to doubt that very shortly after his migration to the Lake country he practically ceased not only to write poetry but to produce any mentionable quantity of *complete* work in the prose form. His mind, no doubt, was incessantly active throughout the whole of the deplorable period upon which we are now entering; but it seems pretty certain that its

activity was not poetic nor even critical, but purely
philosophical, and that the products of that activity went
exclusively to *marginalia* and the pages of note-books.

Yet unfortunately we have almost no evidence, personal or other, from which we can with any certainty
construct the psychological—if one should not rather say
the physiological, or better still, perhaps, the pathological
—history of this cardinal epoch in Coleridge's life. Miss
Wordsworth's diary is nearly silent about him for the
next few years; he was living indeed some dozen miles
from her brother at Grasmere, and they could not
therefore have been in daily intercourse. Southey did
not come to the Lakes till 1803, and the records of his
correspondence only begin therefore from that date.
Mr. Cottle's *Reminiscences* are here a blank; Charles
Lamb's correspondence yields little; and though De
Quincey has plenty to say about this period in his characteristic fashion, it must have been based upon pure
gossip, as he cites no authorities, and did not himself
make Coleridge's acquaintance till six years afterwards.
This, however, is at least certain, that his gloomy
accounts of his own health begin from a period at which
his satisfaction with his new abode was still as fresh as
ever. The house which he had taken, now historic as
the residence of two famous Englishmen, enjoyed a truly
beautiful situation and the command of a most noble
view. It stood in the vale of Derwentwater, on the bank
of the river Greta, and about a mile from the lake.
When Coleridge first entered it, it was uncompleted, and
an arrangement was made by which, after completion, it
was to be divided between the tenant and the landlord,
a Mr. Jackson. As it turned out, however, the then

completed portion was shared by them in common, the
other portion, and eventually the whole, being afterwards
occupied by Southey.

In April 1801, some eight or nine months after his
taking possession of Greta Hall, Coleridge thus describes
it to its future occupant :—

"Our house stands on a low hill, the whole front of
which is one field and an enormous garden, nine-tenths of
which is a nursery garden.   Behind the house is an orchard
and a small wood on a steep slope, at the foot of which is the
river Greta, which winds round and catches the evening's
light in the front of the house.   In front we have a giant
camp—an encamped army of tent-like mountains which, by
an inverted arch, gives a view of another vale.   On our right
the lovely vale and the wedge-shaped lake of Bassenthwaite ;
and on our left Derwentwater and Lodore full in view, and
the fantastic mountains of Borrowdale.   Behind is the
massy Skiddaw, smooth, green, high, with two chasms and
a tent-like ridge in the larger.   A fairer scene you have not
seen in all your wanderings."

There is here no note of discontent with the writer's
surroundings ; and yet, adds Mr. Cuthbert Southey in
his *Life and Correspondence* of his father, the remainder
of this letter was filled by Coleridge with "a most
gloomy account of his health."   Southey writes him in
reply that he is convinced that his friend's "complaint is
gouty, that good living is necessary and a good climate."
In July of the same year he received a visit from
Southey at Greta Hall, and one from Charles and Mary
Lamb in the following summer, and it is probable that
during such intervals of pleasurable excitement his
health and spirits might temporarily rally.   But hence-
forward and until his departure for Malta we gather
nothing from any source as to Coleridge's *normal* condi-

tion of body and mind which is not unfavourable, and
it is quite certain that he had long before 1804 enslaved
himself to that fatal drug which was to remain his
tyrant for the rest of his days.

When, then, and how did this slavery begin ? What
was the precise date of Coleridge's first experiences of
opium, and what the original cause of his taking it ?
Within what time did its use become habitual ? To
what extent was the decline of his health the effect of
the evil habit, and to what, if any, extent its cause ?
And how far, if at all, can the deterioration of his
character and powers be attributed to a decay of
physical constitution, brought about by influences
beyond the sufferer's own control ?

Could every one of these questions be completely
answered, we should be in a position to solve the very
obscure and painful problem before us ; but though
some of them can be answered with more or less
approach to completeness, there is only one of them
which can be finally disposed of.   It is certain, and it
is no doubt matter for melancholy satisfaction to have
ascertained it, that Coleridge first had recourse to opium
as an anodyne.   It was Nature's revolt from pain, and
not her appetite for pleasure, which drove him to the
drug ; and though De Quincey, with his almost comical
malice, remarks that, though Coleridge began in the
desire to obtain relief " there is no proof that he did
not end in voluptuousness," there is on the other hand
no proof whatever that he did so end—*until the habit was
formed*.   It is quite consistent with probability, and
only accords with Coleridge's own express affirmations,
to believe that it was the medicinal efficacy of opium,

and this quality of it alone, which induced him to resort
to it again and again until his senses contracted that
well-known and insatiable craving for the peculiar
excitement, "voluptuous" only to the initiated, which
opium-intoxication creates.   But let Coleridge speak on
this point for himself.   Writing in April 1826 he
says :—

" I wrote a few stanzas three-and-twenty years ago, soon
after my eyes had been opened to the true nature of the
habit into which I had been ignorantly deluded by the
seeming magic effects of opium, in the sudden removal of a
supposed rheumatic affection, attended with swellings in my
knees and palpitation of the heart and pains all over me, by
which I had been bed-ridden for nearly six months.   Unhappily among my neighbours' and landlord's books were a
large number of medical reviews and magazines.   I had
always a fondness (a common case, but most mischievous
turn with reading men who are at all dyspeptic) for dabbling
in medical writings ; and in one of these reviews I met a case
which I fancied very like my own, in which a cure had been
effected by the Kendal Black Drop.   In an evil hour I procured it : it worked miracles—the swellings disappeared,
the pains vanished.   I was all alive, and all around me
being as ignorant as myself, nothing could exceed my
triumph.   I talked of nothing else, prescribed the newly-
discovered panacea for all complaints, and carried a little
about with me not to lose any opportunity of administering
' instant relief and speedy cure ' to all complainers, stranger
or friend, gentle or simple.   Alas ! it is with a bitter
smile, a laugh of gall and bitterness, that I recall this period
of unsuspecting delusion, and how I first became aware of
the Maelstrom, the fatal whirlpool to which I was drawing,
just when the current was beyond my strength to stem.
The state of my mind is truly portrayed in the following
effusion, for God knows ! that from that time I was the
victim of pain and terror, nor had I at any time taken the
flattering poison as a stimulus or for any craving after
pleasurable sensation."

The "effusion" in question has parted company with
the autobiographical note, and the author of the prefatory memoir above quoted conjectures it to have been a
little poem entitled the *Visionary Hope;* but I am myself of opinion, after a careful study of both pieces, that
it is more probably the *Pains of Sleep,* which moreover is
known to have been written in 1803. But whichever it
be, its date is fixed in that year by the statement in the
autobiographical note of 1826 that the stanzas referred
to in it were written "twenty-three years ago." Thus,
then, we have the two facts established, that the opium-
taking habit had its origin in a bodily ailment, and that
at some time in 1803 that habit had become confirmed.
The disastrous experiment in amateur therapeutics,
which was the means of implanting it, could not have
taken place, according to the autobiographical note,
until at least six months after Coleridge's arrival at
Keswick, and perhaps not for some months later yet.
At any rate, it seems tolerably certain that it was
not till the spring of 1801, when the climate of the
Lake country first began to tell unfavourably on his
health, that the "Kendal Black Drop" was taken.
Possibly it may have been about the time (April 1801)
when he wrote the letter to Southey which has been
quoted above, and which, it will be remembered, contained "so gloomy an account of his health." How
painfully ailing he was at this time we know from a
variety of sources, from some of which we also gather
that he must have been a sufferer in more or less serious
forms from his boyhood upwards. Mr. Gillman, for
instance, who speaks on this point with the twofold
authority of confidant and medical expert, records a

statement of Coleridge's to the effect that, as a result of
such schoolboy imprudences as "swimming over the
New River in my clothes and remaining in them, full
half the time from seventeen to eighteen was passed by
me in the sick ward of Christ's Hospital, afflicted with
jaundice and rheumatic fever." From these indiscre-
tions and their consequences "may be dated," Mr. Gillman thinks, "all his bodily sufferings in future life."
That he was a martyr to periodical attacks of rheuma-
tism for some years before his migration to Keswick is
a conclusion resting upon something more than conjecture. The *Ode to the Departing Year* (1796) was written,
as he has himself told us, under a severe attack of rheu-
matism in the head. In 1797 he describes himself in
ill health, and as forced to retire on that account to the
"lonely farmhouse between Porlock and London on the
Exmoor confines of Somerset and Devonshire," where
Kubla Khan was written.[1]

Thus much is, moreover, certain, that whatever were
Coleridge's health and habits during the first two years
of his residence at Keswick, his career as a poet—that
is to say, as a poet of the first order—was closed some
months before that period had expired. The ode entitled *Dejection*, to which reference has so often been
made, was written on the 4th of April 1802, and the
evidential importance which attaches, in connection with
the point under inquiry, to this singularly pathetic

---

[1] Were it not for Coleridge's express statement that he first
took opium at Keswick, one would be inclined to attribute the
gorgeous but formless imagery of that poem to the effects of the
stimulant. It is certainly very like a metrical version of one of
the pleasant variety of opium-dreams described in De Quincey's
poetic prose.

utterance has been almost universally recognised. Coleridge has himself cited its most significant passage in the *Biographia Literaria* as supplying the best description of his mental state at the time when it was written. De Quincey quotes it with appropriate comments in his *Coleridge and Opium-Eating.* Its testimony is reverently invoked by the poet's son in the introductory essay prefixed by him to his edition of his father's works. The earlier stanzas are, however, so necessary to the comprehension of Coleridge's mood at this time that a somewhat long extract must be made. In the opening stanza he expresses a longing that the storm which certain atmospheric signs of a delusively calm evening appear to promise might break forth, so that

> "Those sounds which oft have raised me, whilst they awed,
> And sent my soul abroad,
> Might now perhaps their wonted impulse give,
> Might startle this dull pain, and make it move and live."

And thus, with ever-deepening sadness, the poem proceeds :

> "A grief without a pang, void, dark, and drear,
> A stifled, drowsy, unimpassioned grief,
> Which finds no natural outlet, no relief,
> In word, or sigh, or tear—
> O Lady ! in this wan and heartless mood,
> To other thoughts by yonder throstle woo'd,
> All this long eve, so balmy and serene,
> Have I been gazing on the western sky,
> And its peculiar tint of yellow green :
> And still I gaze—and with how blank an eye !
> And those thin clouds above, in flakes and bars,
> That give away their motion to the stars ;
> Those stars, that glide behind them or between,
> Now sparkling, now bedimmed, but always seen :

H

Yon crescent Moon as fixed as if it grew
In its own cloudless, starless lake of blue ;
I see them all so excellently fair,
I see, not feel how beautiful they are !

　　　" My genial spirits fail,
　　　And what can these avail
To lift the smothering weight from off my breast ?
　　　It were a vain endeavour,
　　　Though I should gaze for ever
On that green light that lingers in the west :
I may not hope from outward forms to win
The passion and the life, whose fountains are within.

" O Lady ! we receive but what we give,
And in our life alone does nature live :
Ours is her wedding garment, ours her shroud !
　　And would we aught behold, of higher worth,
Than that inanimate cold world allowed
To the poor loveless ever-anxious crowd,
　　Ah ! from the soul itself must issue forth,
A light, a glory, a fair luminous cloud
　　　Enveloping the earth—
And from the soul itself must there be sent
　　A sweet and potent voice, of its own birth,
Of all sweet sounds the life and element !

" O pure of heart ! thou need'st not ask of me
What this strong music in the soul may be !
What, and wherein it doth exist,
This light, this glory, this fair luminous mist,
This beautiful and beauty-making power.
　　Joy, virtuous Lady ! Joy that ne'er was given,
Save to the pure, and in their purest hour,
Life, and Life's effluence, cloud at once and shower,
Joy, Lady ! is the spirit and the power,
Which, wedding Nature to us, gives in dower
　　A new Earth and new Heaven,
Undreamt of by the sensual and the proud—
Joy is the sweet voice, Joy the luminous cloud—

We in ourselves rejoice !
And thence flows all that charms or ear or sight,
    All melodies the echoes of that voice,
    All colours a suffusion from that light."

And then follows the much quoted, profoundly touching, deeply significant stanza to which we have referred :—

" There was a time when, though my path was rough,
    This joy within me dallied with distress,
And all misfortunes were but as the stuff
    Whence Fancy made me dreams of happiness :
For hope grew round me, like the twining vine,
And fruits, and foliage, not my own, seemed mine.
But now afflictions bow me down to earth :
Nor care I that they rob me of my mirth,
        But O ! each visitation
Suspends what nature gave me at my birth,
    My shaping spirit of Imagination.
For not to think of what I needs must feel,
    But to be still and patient, all I can ;
And haply by abstruse research to steal
    From my own nature all the natural Man—
    This was my sole resource, my only plan :
Till that which suits a part infects the whole,
And now is almost grown the habit of my Soul."

Sadder lines than these were never perhaps written
by any poet in description of his own feelings. And
what gives them their peculiar sadness—as also, of course,
their special biographical value—is that they are not,
like Shelley's similarly entitled stanzas, the mere expression of a passing mood. They are the record of a
life change, a veritable threnody over a spiritual death.
For there can be no doubt—his whole subsequent history
goes to show it—that Coleridge's "shaping spirit of
Imagination " was in fact dead when these lines were

written.   To a man of stronger moral fibre a renascence
of the poetical instinct in other forms might, as I have
suggested above, been possible ; but the poet of *Christabel*
and the *Ancient Mariner* was dead.   The metaphysician
had taken his place, and was striving, in abstruse research, to live in forgetfulness of the loss.   Little more,
that is to say, than a twelvemonth after the composition
of the second part of *Christabel* the impulse which gave
birth to it had passed away for ever.   Opium-taking had
doubtless begun by this time—may conceivably indeed
have begun nearly a year before—and the mere *mood*
of the poem, the temporary phase of feeling which
directed his mind inwards into deeper reflections on its
permanent state, is no doubt strongly suggestive, in its
excessive depression, of the terrible reaction which is
known to follow upon opium-excitement.   But, I confess, it seems to me improbable that even the habitual
use of the stimulant for so comparatively short a time
as twelve months could have produced so profound a
change in Coleridge's intellectual nature.   I cannot but
think that De Quincey overstates the case in declaring
that "opium killed Coleridge as a poet," though it may
well be that, after the collapse of health, which appears
to me to have been the real *causa causans* in the matter,
had killed the poet as we know him, opium prevented
his resurrection in another and it may be but little inferior form.   On the whole, in fact, the most probable
account of this all-important era in Coleridge's life
appears to me to be this : that in the course of 1801, as
he was approaching his thirtieth year, a distinct change
for the worse—precipitated possibly, as Mr. Gillman
thinks, by the climate of his new place of abode—took

place in his constitution; that his rheumatic habit of
body, and the dyspeptic trouble by which it was
accompanied became confirmed; and that the severe
attacks of the acute form of the malady which he
underwent produced such a permanent lowering of
his vitality and animal spirits as, *first*, to extinguish
the creative impulse, and *then* to drive him to the
physical anodyne of opium and to the mental stimulant
of metaphysics.

From the summer of 1801, at any rate, his *malaise*,
both of mind and body, appears to have grown apace.
Repeated letters from Southey allow us to see how
deeply concerned he was at this time about his friend's
condition. Plans of foreign travel are discussed between
them, and Southey endeavours in vain to spur his
suffering and depressed correspondent to "the assertion
of his supremacy" in some new literary work. But, with
the exception of his occasional contributions to the press,
whatever he committed to paper during these years exists
only, if at all, in a fragmentary form. And his restlessness, continually on the increase, appears by the end of
1802 to have become ungovernable. In November of
that year he eagerly accepted an offer from Thomas
Wedgwood to become his companion on a tour, and he
spent this and the greater part of the following month
in South Wales with some temporary advantage, it
would seem, to his health and spirits. "Coleridge,"
writes Mr. Wedgwood to a friend, "is all kindness to
me, and in prodigious favour here. He is quite easy,
cheerful, and takes great pains to make himself pleasant.
He is willing, indeed desirous, to accompany me to any
part of the globe." "Coll and I," he writes on another

occasion, the abbreviation of name having been suggested to him by Coleridge himself, "harmonise amazingly," and adds that his companion "takes long rambles, and writes a great deal." But the fact that such changes of air and scene produced no permanent effect upon the invalid after his return to his own home appears to show that now, at any rate, his fatal habit had obtained a firm hold upon him. And his " writing a great deal resulted" only in the filling of many note-books, and perhaps the sketching out of many of those vast schemes of literary labour of which he was destined to leave so remarkable a collection at his death. One such we find him forwarding to Southey in the August of 1803— the plan of a Bibliotheca Britannica, or "History of British Literature, bibliographical, biographical, and critical," in eight volumes. The first volume was to contain a "complete history of all Welsh, Saxon, and Erse books that are not translations, but the native growth of Britain ; " to accomplish which, writes Coleridge, "I will with great pleasure join you in learning Welsh and Erse." The second volume was to contain the history of English poetry and poets, including "all prose truly poetical." The third volume "English prose, considered as to style, as to eloquence, as to general impressiveness ; a history of styles and manners, their causes, their birthplace and parentage, their analysis." The fourth volume would take up "the history of metaphysics, theology, medicine, alchemy ; common, canon, and Roman law from Alfred to Henry VII." The fifth would "carry on metaphysics and ethics to the present day in the first half, and comprise in the second half the theology of all the reformers." In the sixth and

seventh volumes were to be included "all the articles
you (Southey) can get on all the separate arts and
sciences that have been treated of in books since the
Reformation; and by this time," concludes the enthusiastic projector, "the book, if it answered at all, would
have gained so high a reputation that you need not fear
having whom you liked to write the different articles—
medicine, surgery, chemistry, etc.; navigation, travellers'
voyages, etc., etc." There is certainly a melancholy
humour in the formulation of so portentous a scheme by
a man who was at this moment wandering aimlessly
among the lakes and mountains, unable to settle down
to any definite piece of literary work, or even to throw
off a fatal habit, which could not fail, if persevered in, to
destroy all power of steady application in the future.
That neither the comic nor the pathetic element in the
situation was lost upon Southey is evident from his half-
sad, half-satirical, wholly winning reply. "Your plan,"
he writes, "is too good, too gigantic, quite beyond my
powers. If you had my tolerable state of health and
that love of steady and productive employment which
is now grown into a necessary habit with me, if you
were to execute and would execute it, it would be
beyond all doubt the most valuable work of any age or
any country; but I cannot fill up such an outline. No
man can better feel where he fails than I do, and to
rely upon you for whole quartos! Dear Coleridge, the
smile that comes with that thought is a very melancholy
one; and if Edith saw me now she would think my eyes
were weak again, when in truth the humour that covers
them springs from another cause." A few weeks after
this interchange of correspondence Coleridge was once

again to prove how far he was from possessing Southey's
"tolerable state of health." Throughout the whole of
this year he had been more restless than ever. In
January 1803 we find him staying with Southey at
Bristol, " suffering terribly from the climate, and talking
of going abroad." A week later he is at Stowey, plan-
ning schemes, not destined to be realised, of foreign
travel with Wedgwood. Returning again to Keswick, he
started, after a few months' quiescence, on 15th August,
in company with Wordsworth and his sister, for a tour
in Scotland, but after a fortnight he found himself too
ill to proceed. The autumn rains set in, and "poor
Coleridge," writes Miss Wordsworth, "being very
unwell, determined to send his clothes to Edinburgh,
and make the best of his way thither, being afraid to
face much wet weather in an open carriage." It is
possible, however, that his return to Keswick may have
been hastened by the circumstance that Southey, who
had paid a brief visit to the Lake country two years
before, was expected in a few days at the house which
was destined to be his abode for the longest portion of
his life. He arrived at Greta Hall on 7th September
1803, and from time to time during the next six months
his correspondence gives us occasional glimpses of
Coleridge's melancholy state. At the end of December,
his health growing steadily worse, he conceived the project of a voyage to Madeira, and quitted Keswick with
the intention, after paying a short visit to the Wordsworths, of betaking himself to London to make prepara-
tions. His stay at Grasmere, however, was longer than
he had counted on. " He was detained for a month by a
severe attack of illness, induced, if his description is to

be relied on, by the use of narcotics.[1] Unsuspicious of
the cause, Mrs. and Miss Wordsworth nursed him with
the tenderest affection, while the poet himself, usually a
parsimonious man, forced upon him, to use Coleridge's
own words, a hundred pounds in the event of his going
to Madeira, and his friend Stuart offered to befriend
him." From Grasmere he went to Liverpool, where he
spent a pleasant week with his old Unitarian friend, Dr.
Crompton, and arrived in London at the close of 1803.
Here, however, his plans were changed.   Malta was
substituted for Madeira, in response to an invitation from
his friend Mr., afterwards Sir John, Stoddart, then
resident as judge in the Mediterranean island.   By 12th
March, as we gather from the Southey correspondence,
the change of arrangements had been made.   Two days
afterwards he receives a letter of valediction from his
"old friend and brother" at Greta Hall, and on 2d April
1804, he sailed from England in the *Speedwell*, dropping
anchor sixteen days later in Valetta harbour.

[1] See Miss Meteyard (*A Group of Englishmen*, p. 223). Her
evidence, however, on any point otherwise doubtful in Coleridge's
history should be received with caution, as her estimate of the
poet certainly errs somewhat on the side of excessive harshness.

CHAPTER VI.

[1806-1809.]

NEVER was human being destined so sadly and signally
to illustrate the *cœlum non animum* aphorism as the
unhappy passenger on the *Speedwell*. Southey shall
describe his condition when he left England; and
his own pathetic lines to William Wordsworth will
picture him to us on his return. "You are in great
measure right about Coleridge," writes the former to
his friend Rickman, "he is worse in body than you
seem to believe; but the main cause lies in his own
management of himself, or rather want of management.
His mind is in a perpetual St. Vitus's dance—eternal
activity without action. At times he feels mortified
that he should have done so little, but this feeling never
produces any exertion. 'I will begin to-morrow,' he
says, and thus he has been all his lifelong letting to-day
slip. He has had no heavy calamities in life, and so
contrives to be miserable about trifles. Poor fellow,
there is no one thing which gives me so much pain as

the witnessing such a waste of unequalled powers."
Then, after recalling the case of a highly promising
schoolfellow, who had made shipwreck of his life, and
whom "a few individuals only remember with a sort of
horror and affection, which just serves to make them
melancholy whenever they think of him or mention his
name," he adds : "This will not be the case with
Coleridge ; the *disjecta membra* will be found if he does
not die early : but having so much to do, so many errors
to weed out of the world which he is capable of eradi-
cating, if he does die without doing his work, it would
half break my heart, for no human being has had more
talents allotted." Such being his closest friend's account
of him, and knowing, as we now do (what Southey perhaps had no suspicion of at the time), the chief if not the
sole or original cause of his morally nerveless condition,
it is impossible not to feel that he did the worst possible
thing for himself in taking this journey to Malta. In
quitting England he cut himself off from those last
possibilities of self-conquest which the society and
counsels of his friends might otherwise have afforded
him, and the consequences were, it is to be feared,
disastrous. After De Quincey's incredibly cool assertion
that it was "notorious that Coleridge began the use of
opium, not as a relief from any bodily pain or nervous
irritations, since his constitution was strong and excellent (!), but as a source of luxurious sensations," we
must receive anything which he has to say on this
particular point with the utmost caution ; but there is
only too much plausibility in his statement that, Coleridge being necessarily thrown, while at Malta, "a good
deal upon his own resources in the narrow society of a

garrison, he there confirmed and cherished . . . his habit of taking opium in large quantities." Contrary to his expectations, moreover, the Maltese climate failed to benefit him. At first, indeed, he did experience some feeling of relief, but afterwards, according to Mr. Gillman, he spoke of his rheumatic limbs as "lifeless tools," and of the "violent pains in his bowels, which neither opium, ether, nor peppermint combined could relieve."

Occupation, however, was not wanting to him, if occupation could have availed in the then advanced stage of his case. He early made the acquaintance of the governor of the island, Sir Alexander Ball, who, having just lost his secretary by death, requested Coleridge to undertake that official's duties until his successor should be appointed. By this arrangement the governor and the public service in all likelihood profited more than the provisional secretary; for Coleridge's literary abilities proved very serviceable in the department of diplomatic correspondence. The dignities of the office, Mr. Gillman tells us, no doubt on Coleridge's own authority, "he never attempted to support; he was greatly annoyed at what he thought its unnecessary parade, and he petitioned Sir Alexander Ball to be relieved from it." The purely mechanical duties of the post, too, appear to have troubled him. He complains, in one of the journals which he kept during this period, of having been "for months past incessantly employed in official tasks, subscribing, examining, administering oaths, auditing, etc." On the whole it would seem that the burden of his secretarial employment, though doubtless it would have been found light enough by any one accustomed to public business, was rather a weariness

to the flesh than a distraction to the mind ; while in the
meantime a new symptom of disorder—a difficulty of
breathing, to which he was always afterwards subject—
began to manifest itself in his case.   Probably he was
glad enough—relieved, in more than one sense of the
word—when, in the autumn of 1805, the new secretary
arrived at Malta to take his place.

On 27th September Coleridge quitted the island on
his homeward journey *viâ* Italy, stopping for a short
time at Syracuse on his way.   At Naples, which he
reached on the 15th of December, he made a longer stay,
and in Rome his sojourn lasted some months.   Unfortunately, for a reason which will presently appear, there
remains no written record of his impressions of the
Eternal City ; and though Mr. Gillman assures us that
the gap is "partly filled by his own verbal account,
repeated at various times to the writer of this memoir,"
the public of to-day is only indebted to "the writer of
this memoir" for the not very startling information that
Coleridge, "while in Rome, was actively employed in
visiting the great works of art, statues, pictures, build-
ings, palaces, etc. etc., observations on which he minuted
down for publication."   It is somewhat more interesting
to learn that he made the acquaintance of many literary
and artistic notabilities at that time congregated there,
including Tieck, the German poet and novelist, and the
American painter Alston, to whose skill we owe what is
reputed to be the best of his many not easily reconcilable portraits.   The loss of his Roman memoranda was
indirectly brought about by a singular incident, his
account of which has met with some undeserved ridicule
at the hands of Tory criticism.   When about to quit

Rome for England *viâ* Switzerland and Germany he took the precaution of inquiring of Baron von Humboldt, brother of the traveller, and then Prussian Minister at the Court of Rome, whether the proposed route was safe, and was by him informed that he would do well to keep out of the reach of Bonaparte, who was meditating the seizure of his person. According to Coleridge, indeed, an order for his arrest had actually been transmitted to Rome, and he was only saved from its execution by the connivance of the "good old Pope," Pius VII., who sent him a passport and counselled his immediate flight. Hastening to Leghorn, he discovered an American vessel ready to sail for England, on board of which he embarked. On the voyage she was chased by a French vessel, which so alarmed the captain that he compelled Coleridge to throw his papers, including these precious MSS., overboard. The wrath of the First Consul against him was supposed to have been excited by his contributions to the *Morning Post*, an hypothesis which De Quincey reasonably finds by no means so ridiculous as it appeared to a certain writer in *Blackwood*, who treated it as the "very consummation of moon-struck vanity," and compared it to "John Dennis's frenzy in retreating from the sea-coast under the belief that Louis XIV. had commissioned commissaries to land on the English shore and make a dash at his person." It must be remembered, however, that Mr. Fox, to whose statement on such a point Napoleon would be likely to attach especial weight, had declared in the House of Commons that the rupture of the Peace of Amiens had been brought about by certain essays in the *Morning Post*, and there is certainly no reason to believe that a tyrant whose animosity against literary or quasi-literary assailants ranged from Madame de Staël down to the bookseller Palm would have regarded a man of Coleridge's reputation in letters as beneath the stoop of his vengeance.

After an absence of two years and a half Coleridge arrived in England in August 1806. That his then condition of mind and body was a profoundly miserable one, and that he himself was acutely conscious of it, will be seen later on in certain extracts from his correspondence; but his own *Lines to William Wordsworth*—lines "composed on the night after his recitation of a poem on the growth of an individual mind"—contain an even more tragic expression of his state. It was Wordsworth's pensive retrospect of their earlier years together which awoke the bitterest pangs of self-reproach in his soul, and wrung from it the cry which follows :—

> " Ah ! as I listened with a heart forlorn
> The pulses of my being beat anew :
> And even as life returns upon the drowned,
> Life's joy rekindling roused a throng of pains—
> Keen pangs of Love, awakening as a babe
> Turbulent, with an outcry in the heart ;
> And fears self-willed, that shunned the eye of hope ;
> And hope that scarce would know itself from fear ;
> Sense of past youth, and manhood come in vain,
> And genius given, and knowledge won in vain ;
> And all which I had culled in wood-walks wild,
> And all which patient toil had reared, and all,
> Commune with thee had opened out—but flowers
> Strewn on my corse, and borne upon my bier,
> In the same coffin, for the self-same grave !"

A dismal and despairing strain indeed, but the situation unhappily was not less desperate. We are, in fact, entering upon that period of Coleridge's life — a period, roughly speaking, of about ten years — which no admirer of his genius, no lover of English letters, no one, it might even be said, who wishes to think well of human nature, can ever contemplate without pain. His history from the day of his landing in England in August 1806 till the day when he entered Mr. Gillman's house in 1816 is one long and miserable story of self-indulgence and self-reproach, of lost opportunities, of neglected duties, of unfinished undertakings. His movements and his occupation for the first year after his return are not now traceable with exactitude, but his time was apparently spent partly in London and partly at Grasmere and Keswick. When in London, Mr. Stuart, who had now become proprietor of the *Courier*, allowed him to occupy rooms at the office of that newspaper to save him expense; and Coleridge, though his regular connection with the *Courier* did not begin till some years afterwards, may possibly have repaid the accommodation by occasional contributions or by assistance to its editor in some other form. It seems certain, at any rate, that if he was earning no income in this way he was earning none at all. His friend and patron, Mr. Thomas Wedgwood, had died while he was in Malta; but the full pension of £150 per annum bestowed upon him by the two brothers jointly continued to be paid to him by Josiah, the senior. Coleridge, however, had landed in England in ignorance of his patron's death. He had wholly neglected to keep up any correspondence with the Wedgwoods during his stay in Malta, and though "dreadfully affected" by it, as Mr. Poole records, he seems to have allowed nearly a year to elapse before communicating with the surviving brother. The letter which he then wrote deserves quotation, not only as testimony to his physical and pecuniary condition on his arrival in England, but as affording a distressing picture of the morbid state of his emotions and the enfeebled condition of his will. "As to the reasons for my silence, they are," he incoherently begins, "impossible, and the numbers of the *causes* of it, with the almost weekly expectation for the last eight months of receiving my books, manuscripts, etc. from Malta, has been itself a cause of increasing the procrastination which constant ill health, despondency, domestic distractions, and embarrassment from accidents, equally unconnected with my will or conduct" [every cause mentioned, it will be seen, but the true one], "had already seated deep in my very muscles, as it were. I do not mean to accuse myself of idleness—I have enough of self-crimination without adding imaginary articles—but in all things that affect my moral feelings I have sunk under such a strange cowardice of pain that I have not unfrequently kept letters from persons dear to me for weeks together unopened. After a most miserable passage from Leghorn of fifty-five days, during which my life was twice given over, I found myself again in my native country, ill, penniless, and worse than homeless. I had been near a month in the country before I ventured or could summon courage enough to ask a question concerning you and yours, and yet God Almighty knows that every hour the thought had been gnawing at my heart. I then for the first time heard of that event which sounded like my own knell, without its natural hope or sense of rest. Such shall I be (is the thought that

I

haunts me), but O! not such; O! with what a different retrospect! But I owe it to justice to say, Such good I truly can do myself, etc., etc." The rest of this painfully inarticulate letter is filled with further complaints of ill health, with further protestations of irresponsibility for the neglect of duties, and with promises, never to be fulfilled, of composing or assisting others to compose a memoir of Thomas Wedgwood, who, in addition to his general repute as a man of culture, had made a special mark by his speculations in psychology.

The singular expression, "worse than homeless," and the reference to domestic distractions, appear to indicate that some estrangement had already set in between Coleridge and his wife. De Quincey's testimony to its existence at the time (a month or so later) when he made Coleridge's acquaintance may, subject to the usual deductions, be accepted as trustworthy; and, of course, for aught we know, it may then have been already of some years' standing. That the provocation to it on the husband's part may be so far antedated is at least a reasonable conjecture. There may be nothing—in all likelihood there is nothing—worth attention in De Quincey's gossip about the young lady, "intellectually very much superior to Mrs. Coleridge, who became a neighbour and daily companion of Coleridge's walks" at Keswick. But if there be no foundation for his remarks on "the mischiefs of a situation which exposed Mrs. Coleridge to an invidious comparison with a more intellectual person," there is undoubtedly plenty of point in the immediately following observation that "it was most unfortunate for Coleridge himself to be continually compared with one so ideally correct and regular in his habits as Mr. Southey."

The passion of female jealousy assuredly did not need
to be called into play to account for the alienation of
Mrs. Coleridge from her husband. Mrs. Carlyle has
left on record her pathetic lament over the fate of a
woman who marries a man of genius ; but a man of
genius of the coldly selfish and exacting type of the
Chelsea philosopher would probably be a less severe
burden to a woman of housewifely instincts than the
weak, unmethodical, irresolute, shiftless being that Coleridge had by this time become. After the arrival of
the Southeys, Mrs. Coleridge would indeed have been
more than human if she had not looked with an envious
eye upon the contrast between her sister Edith's lot and
her own. For this would give her the added pang of
perceiving that she was specially unlucky in the matter,
and that men of genius could ("if they chose," as she
would probably, though not perhaps quite justly have
put it) make very good husbands indeed. If one poet
could finish his poems, and pay his tradesmen's bills,
and work steadily for the publishers in his own house
without the necessity of periodical flittings to various
parts of the United Kingdom or the Continent, why, so
could another. With such reflections as these Mrs.
Coleridge's mind was no doubt sadly busy during the
early years of her residence at the Lakes, and, since their
causes did not diminish but rather increased in intensity
as time went on, the estrangement between them—or
rather, to do Coleridge justice, her estrangement from
her husband—had, by 1806, no doubt become complete.
The fatal habit which even up to this time seems to
have been unknown to most of his friends could hardly
have been a secret to his wife, and his four or five

years of slavery to it may well have worn out her patience.

This single cause indeed, namely, Coleridge's addiction to opium, is quite sufficient, through the humiliations, discomfort, and privations, pecuniary and otherwise, for which the vice was no doubt mediately or immediately responsible, to account for the unhappy issue of a union which undoubtedly was one of love to begin with, and which seems to have retained that character for at least six years of its course. We have noted the language of warm affection in which the "beloved Sara" is spoken of in the early poems, and up to the time of Coleridge's stay in Germany his feelings towards his wife remained evidently unchanged. To his children, of whom three out of the four born to him had survived, he was deeply attached ; and the remarkable promise displayed by the eldest son, Hartley, and his youngest child and only daughter, Sara, made them objects of no less interest to his intellect than to his heart. "Hartley," he writes to Mr. Poole in 1803, "is a strange, strange boy, exquisitely wild, an utter visionary ; like the moon among thin clouds, he moves in a circle of light of his own making. He alone is a light of his own." And of his daughter in the same poetic strain : "My meek little Sara is a remarkably interesting baby, with the finest possible skin, and large blue eyes, and she smiles as if she were basking in a sunshine as mild as moonlight of her own quiet happiness." Derwent, a less remarkable but no less attractive child than his brother and sister (whom he was destined long to survive), held an equal place in his father's affections. Yet all these interwoven influences—a deep love of his children and a sincere

attachment to his wife, of whom, indeed, he never ceased
to speak with respect and regard—were as powerless as
in so many thousands of other cases they have been, to
brace an enfeebled will to the task of self-reform.   In
1807 "respect and regard" had manifestly taken the
place of any warmer feeling in his mind.   Later on in
the letter above quoted he says, " In less than a week I
go down to Ottery, with my children and their mother,
from a sense of duty" (*i.e.* to his brother, the Rev.
George Coleridge, who had succeeded his father as head
master of the Ottery St. Mary Grammar School) " as
far as it affects myself, and from a promise made to Mrs.
Coleridge, as far as it affects her, and indeed of a debt
of respect to her for her many praiseworthy qualities."
When husbands and wives take to liquidating debts
of this kind, and in this spirit, it is pretty conclusive
evidence that all other accounts between them are
closed.

The letter from which these extracts have been taken
was written from Aisholt near Bridgewater, where Coleridge was then staying, with his wife and children, as
the guest of a Mr. Price ; and his friend Poole's description to Josiah Wedgwood of his state at that time is
significant as showing that some at least of his intimate
acquaintances had no suspicion of the real cause of his
bodily and mental disorders.   "I admire him," Poole
writes, " and pity him more than ever.   His information
is much extended, the *great* qualities of his mind
heightened and better disciplined, but alas ! his health
is much weaker, and his great failing, procrastination, or
the incapability of acting agreeably to his wish and will,
much increased."

Whether the promised visit to Ottery St. Mary was ever paid there is no record to show, but at the end of July 1807 we again hear of the Coleridges at the house of a Mr. Chubb, a descendant of the Deist, at Bridgewater; and here it was that De Quincey, after having endeavoured in vain to run the poet to earth at Stowey, where he had been staying with Mr. Poole, and whence he had gone to pay a short visit to Lord Egmont, succeeded in obtaining an introduction to him. The characteristic passage in which the younger man describes their first meeting is too long for quotation, and it is to be hoped too well known to need it: his vivid and acute criticism of Coleridge's conversation may be more appropriately cited hereafter. His evidence as to the conjugal relations of Coleridge and his wife has been already discussed; and the last remaining point of interest about this memorable introduction is the testimony which it incidentally affords to De Quincey's genuine and generous instinct of hero-worship, and to the depth of Coleridge's pecuniary embarrassments. The loan of £300, which the poet's enthusiastic admirer insisted on Cottle's conveying to him as from an unknown "young man of fortune who admired his talents," should cover a multitude of De Quincey's subsequent sins. It was indeed only upon Cottle's urgent representation that he had consented to reduce the sum from £500 to £300. Nor does there seem any doubt of his having honestly attempted to conceal his own identity with the nameless benefactor, though, according to his own later account, he failed.[1]

---

[1] " In a letter written by him (Coleridge) about fifteen years after that time, I found that he had become aware of all the circumstances, perhaps through some indiscretion of Mr. Cottle's."

This occurred in November 1807, and in the previous month De Quincey had been able to render Coleridge a minor service, while at the same moment gratifying a long cherished wish of his own. Mrs. Coleridge was about to return with her children to Keswick, but her husband, not yet master of this £300 windfall, and undoubtedly at his wits' end for money, was arranging for a course of lectures to be delivered at the Royal Institution early in the ensuing year, and could not accompany them. De Quincey offered accordingly to be their escort, and duly conducted them to Wordsworth's house, thus making the acquaintance of the second of his two great poetical idols within a few months of paying his first homage to the other. In February 1808 Coleridge again took up his abode in London at his old free quarters in the *Courier* office, and began the delivery of a promised series of sixteen lectures on Poetry and the Fine Arts. "I wish you could see him," again writes Poole to Wedgwood, "you would pity and admire. He is much improved, but has still less voluntary power than ever. Yet he is so committed that I think he must deliver these lectures." Considering that the authorities of the Royal Institution had agreed to pay him one hundred guineas for delivering the lectures, he undoubtedly was more or less "committed;" and his voluntary power, however small, might be safely supposed to be equal to the task of fulfilling a contract. But to get the lecturer into the lecture-room does not amount to much more than bringing the horse to the water. You can no more make the one drink than you

Perhaps, however, no very great indiscretion on Mr. Cottle's part was needed to enable Coleridge to trace the loan to so ardent a young admirer and disciple.

can prevent the other from sending his audience away thirsty. Coleridge's lectures on Poetry and the Fine Arts were confused, ill arranged, and generally disappointing to the last degree. Sometimes it was not even possible to bring the horse to the water. Charles Lamb writes to Manning on the 20th of February 1808 (early days indeed) that Coleridge had only delivered two lectures, and that though " two more were intended, he did not come." De Quincey writes of " dismissals of audience after audience, with pleas of illness; and on many of his lecture-days I have seen all Albemarle Street closed by a lock of carriages filled with women of distinction, until the servants of the Institution or their own footmen advanced to the carriage-doors with the intelligence that Mr. Coleridge had been suddenly taken ill." Naturally there came a time when the "women of distinction" began to tire of this treatment. "The plea, which at first had been received with expressions of concern, repeated too often began to rouse disgust. Many in anger, and some in real uncertainty whether it would not be trouble thrown away, ceased to attend." And what De Quincey has to say of the lectures themselves when they did by chance get delivered is no less melancholy. "The lecturer's appearance," he says, "was generally that of a man struggling with pain and overmastering illness."

"His lips were baked with feverish heat, and often black in colour ; and in spite of the water which he continued drinking through the whole course of the lecture, he often seemed to labour under an almost paralytic inability to raise the upper jaw from the lower " [*i.e.* I suppose to move the lower jaw]. "In such a state it is clear that nothing could save the lecture itself from reflecting his own feebleness and exhaustion except the advantage of having been precomposed in some happier mood. But that never happened : most unfortunately, he relied on his extempore ability to carry him through. Now, had he been in spirits, or had he gathered animation and kindled by his own emotion, no written lecture could have been more effectual than one of his unpremeditated colloquial harangues. But either he was depressed originally below the point from which reascent was possible, or else this reaction was intercepted by continual disgust from looking back upon his own ill success ; for assuredly he never once recovered that free and eloquent movement of thought which he could command at any time in a private company. The passages he read, moreover, in illustrating his doctrines, were generally unhappily chosen, because chosen at haphazard, from the difficulty of finding at a moment's summons these passages which his purpose required. Nor do I remember any that produced much effect except two or three which I myself put ready marked into his hands among the *Metrical Romances*, edited by Ritson. Generally speaking, the selections were as injudicious and as inappropriate as they were ill delivered, for among Coleridge's accomplishments good reading was not one. He had neither voice (so at least I thought) nor management of voice. This defect is unfortunate in a public lecturer, for it is inconceivable how much weight and effectual pathos can be communicated by sonorous depth and melodious cadence of the human voice to sentiments the most trivial ; [1] nor, on the other hand, how the grandest are emasculated by a style of reading which fails in distributing the lights and shadows of a musical intonation. However, this defect chiefly concerned the immediate impression ; the most afflicting to a friend of Coleridge's was the entire absence of his own peculiar and majestic intellect ; no heart, no soul, was in anything he said ; no strength of feeling in recalling univer-

---

[1] The justice of this criticism will be acknowledged by those many persons whom Mr. Bright's great elocutionary skill has occasionally deluded into imagining that the very commonplace verse which the famous orator has been often known to quote with admiration is poetry of a high order.

sal truths, no power of originality or compass of moral relations in his novelties,—all was a poor, faint reflection from pearls once scattered on the highway by himself in the prodigality of his early opulence—a mendicant dependence on the alms dropped from his own overflowing treasury of happier times."

Severe as is this censure of the lectures, there is unhappily no good ground for disputing its substantial justice. And the inferences which it suggests are only too painfully plain. One can well understand Coleridge's being an ineffective lecturer, and no failure in this respect, however conspicuous, would necessarily force us to the hypothesis of physical disability. But a Coleridge who could no more *compose* a lecture than he could deliver one—a Coleridge who could neither write nor extemporise anything specially remarkable on a subject so congenial to him as that of English poetry— must assuredly have spent most of his time, whether in the lecture-room or out of it, in a state of incapacity for sustained intellectual effort. De Quincey's humorous account of the lecturer's shiftless untidy life at the *Courier* office, and even the Rabelaisian quip which Charles Lamb throws at it in the above-quoted letter to Manning, are sufficient indications of his state at this time. "Oh, Charles," he writes to Lamb, early in February, just before the course of lectures was to begin, "I am very, very ill. *Vixi.*" The sad truth is that, as seems to have been always the case with him when living alone, he was during these months of his residence in London more constantly and hopelessly under the dominion of opium than ever.

CHAPTER VII.

Return to the Lakes — From Keswick to Grasmere — With
Wordsworth at Allan Bank — The *Friend* — Quits the
Lake country for ever.

[1809-1810.]

FROM the close of this series of lectures in the month of
May 1808 until the end of the year it is impossible to
trace Coleridge's movements or even to determine the
nature of his occupation with any approach to exactitude.
The probability is, however, that he remained in London
at his lodgings in the *Courier* office, and that he sup-
ported himself by rendering assistance in various ways
to Mr. Daniel Stuart. We know nothing of him, however, with certainty until we find him once more at the
Lakes in the early part of the year 1809, but not in his
own home. Wordsworth had removed from his former
abode at Grasmere to Allan Bank, a larger house some
three-quarters of a mile distant, and there Coleridge
took up his residence, more, it would seem, as a permanent inmate of his friend's house than as a guest.
The specific cause of this migration from Greta Hall to
Allan Bank does not appear, but all the accessible
evidence, contemporary and subsequent, seems to point

to the probability that it was the result of a definite
break-up of Coleridge's own home. He continued, at
any rate, to reside in Wordsworth's house during the
whole seven months of his editorship of the *Friend*, a
new venture in periodical literature which he undertook
at this period; and we shall see that upon its failure he
did not resume his residence at Greta Hall, but quitted
the Lake country at once and for ever.

We need not take too literally Coleridge's declaration
in the *Biographia Literaria* that one "main object of his
in starting the *Friend* was to establish the philosophical
distinction between the Reason and the Understanding."
Had this been so, or at least had the periodical been
actually conducted in conformity with any such purpose,
even the chagrined projector himself could scarcely have
had the face to complain, as Coleridge did very bitterly,
of the reception accorded to it by the public. The most
unpractical of thinkers can hardly have imagined that
the "general reader" would "take in" a weekly metaphysical journal published at a town in Cumberland.
The *Friend* was not quite so essentially hopeless an enterprise as that would have been; but the accidents of
mismanagement and imprudence soon made it, for all
practical purposes, sufficiently desperate. Even the
forlorn *Watchman*, which had been set on foot when
Coleridge had fourteen years' less experience of the world,
was hardly more certainly foredoomed. The first care
of the founder of the *Friend* was to select, as the place
of publication, a town exactly twenty-eight miles from
his own abode—a distance virtually trebled, as De Quincey
observes, "by the interposition of Kirkstone, a mountain
only to be scaled by a carriage ascent of three miles,

and so steep in parts that without four horses no solitary
traveller can persuade the neighbouring innkeepers to
convey him." Here, however, at Penrith, "by way of
purchasing intolerable difficulties at the highest price,"
Coleridge was advised and actually persuaded to set up
a printer, to buy and lay in a stock of paper, types, etc.,
instead of resorting to some printer already established
at a nearer place—as, for instance, Kendal, which was ten
miles nearer, and connected with Coleridge's then place
of residence by a daily post, whereas at Penrith there
was no post at all. Having thus studiously and
severely handicapped himself, the projector of the
new periodical set to work, upon the strength of what
seems to have been in great measure a fancy list of
subscribers, to print and, so far as his extraordinary
arrangements permitted, to circulate his journal. With
naïve sententiousness he warns the readers of the
Biographia Literaria against trusting, in their own case,
to such a guarantee as he supposed himself to possess.
"You cannot," he observes, "be certain that the names
on a subscription list have been put down by sufficient
authority; or, should that be ascertained, it still remains
to be known whether they were not extorted by some
over-zealous friend's importunity; whether the subscriber
had not yielded his name merely from want of courage
to say no! and with the intention of dropping the work
as soon as possible." Thus out of a hundred patrons
who had been obtained for the *Friend* by an energetic
canvasser, "ninety threw up the publication before the
fourth number without any notice, though it was well
known to them that in consequence of the distance and
the slowness and irregularity of the conveyance" [it is

amusing to observe the way in which Coleridge notes
these drawbacks of his own creation as though they were
"the act of God"] "I was compelled to lay in a stock
of stamped paper for at least eight weeks beforehand,
each sheet of which stood me in fivepence previous to its
arrival at my printer's; though the subscription money
was not to be received till the twenty-first week after the
commencement of the work; and, lastly, though it was
in nine cases out of ten impracticable for me to receive
the money for two or three numbers without paying an
equal sum for the postage."

Enough appears in this undesignedly droll account of
the venture to show pretty clearly that, even had the
Friend obtained a reasonable measure of popularity at
starting, the flagrant defects in the methods of distributing and financing it must have insured its early decease.
But, as a matter of fact, it had no chance of popularity
from the outset. Its first number appeared on 1st August
1809, and Coleridge, writing to Southey on 20th October
of the same year, speaks of his "original apprehension" that the plan and execution of the *Friend* is so
utterly unsuitable to the public taste as to preclude all
rational hopes of its success. "Much," he continues,
"might have been done to have made the former
numbers less so, by the interposition of others written
more expressly for general interest;" and he promises
to do his best in future to "interpose tales and whole
numbers of amusement, which will make the periods
lighter and shorter." Meanwhile he begs Southey to
write a letter to the *Friend* in a lively style, rallying its
editor on "his Quixotism in expecting that the public will
ever pretend to understand his lucubrations or feel any

interest in subjects of such sad and unkempt antiquity."
Southey, ever good-natured, complied, even amid the
unceasing press of his work, with the request; and to
the letter of lightly-touched satire which he contributed
to the journal he added a few private lines of friendly
counsel, strongly urging Coleridge to give two or three
amusing numbers, and he would hear of admiration on
every side. "Insert too," he suggested, "a few more
poems—any that you have, except *Christabel*, for that is
of too much value. And write *now* that character of
Bonaparte, announced in former times for 'to-morrow,
and to-morrow, and to-morrow.'" It was too late, however, for good advice to be of any avail: the *Friend* was
past praying for. It lingered on till its twenty-eighth
number, and expired, unlike the *Watchman*, without any
farewell to its friends, in the third week of March 1810.

The republication of this periodical, or rather selections from it, which appeared in 1818, is hardly perhaps
described with justice in De Quincey's words as "altogether and absolutely a new work." A reader can, at
any rate, form a pretty fair estimate from it of the style
and probable public attractions of the original issue;
and a perusal of it, considered in its character as a bid
for the patronage of the general reader, is certainly
calculated to excite an astonishment too deep for words.
We have, of course, to bear in mind that the standard
of the readable in our grandfathers' days was a more
liberal and tolerant one than it is in our own. In those
days of leisurely communications and slowly moving
events there was relatively at least a far larger public
for a weekly issue of moral and philosophical essays,
under the name of a periodical, than it would be found

easy to secure at present, when even a monthly discourse upon things in general requires Mr. Ruskin's
brilliancy of eloquence, vivacity of humour, and perpetual charm of unexpectedness to carry it off. Still
the *Spectator* continued to be read in Coleridge's day,
and people therefore must have had before them a
perpetual example of what it was possible to do in the
way of combining entertainment with instruction. How,
then, it could have entered into the mind of the most
sanguine projector to suppose that the *longueurs* and the
difficulty of the *Friend* would be patiently borne with
for the sake of the solid nutriment which it contained it is
quite impossible to understand. Even supposing that a
weekly, whose avowed object was "to aid in the formation of fixed principles in politics, morals, and religion,"
could possibly be floated, even "with literary amusements interspersed," it is evident that very much would
depend upon the character of these "amusements" themselves. In the republication of 1817 they appear under
the heading of "landing-places." One of them consists
of a parallel between Voltaire and Erasmus, and between
Rousseau and Luther, founded, of course, on the respective attitudes of the two pairs of personages to the
Revolution and the Reformation. Another at the end
of the series consists of a criticism of, and panegyric on,
Sir Alexander Ball, the governor of Malta. Such are
the landing-places. But how should any reader, wearied
with "for ever climbing up the climbing wave" of
Coleridge's eloquence, have found rest or refreshment on
one of these uncomfortable little sandbanks? It was
true that the original issue of the *Friend* contained
poetical contributions which do not appear in the re-

publication; but poetry in itself, or, at any rate, good poetry, is not a relief to the overstrained faculties, and, even if it were, the relief would have been provided at too infrequent intervals to affect the general result. The fact is, however, that Coleridge's own theory of his duty as a public instructor was in itself fatal to any hope of his venture proving a commercial success. Even when entreated by Southey to lighten the character of the periodical, he accompanies his admission of the worldly wisdom of the advice with something like a protest against such a departure from the severity of his original plan. His object, as he puts it with much cogency from his own unpractical point of view— his object being to teach men how to think on politics, religion, and morals, and thinking being a very arduous and distasteful business to the mass of mankind, it followed that the essays of the *Friend* (and particularly the earlier essays, in which the reader required to be "grounded" in his subject) could hardly be agreeable reading. With perfect frankness indeed does he admit in his prospectus that he must "submit to be thought dull by those who seek amusement only." He hoped, however, as he says in one of his earlier essays, to become livelier as he went on. "The proper merit of a foundation is its massiveness and solidity. The conveniences and ornaments, the gilding and stucco-work, the sunshine and sunny prospects, will come with the superstructure." But the building, alas! was never destined to be completed, and the architect had his own misgivings about the attractions even of the completed edifice. "I dare not flatter myself that any endeavours of mine, compatible with the duty I owe to

K

the truth and the hope of permanent utility, will render
the *Friend* agreeable to the majority of what is called
the reading public. I never expected it. How indeed
could I when, etc." Yet, in spite of these profes-
sions, it is clear from the prospectus that Coleridge
believed in the possibility of obtaining a public for the
Friend. He says that " a motive for honourable ambition
was supplied by the fact that every periodical paper of
the kind now attempted, which had been conducted
with zeal and ability, was not only well received at the
time, but has become popular ; " and he seems to regard
it as a comparatively unimportant circumstance that the
Friend would be distinguished from "its celebrated predecessors, the *Spectator* and the like," by the "greater
length of the separate essays, by their closer connection
with each other, and by the predominance of one object,
and the common bearing of all to one end." It was, of
course, exactly this *plus* of prolixity and *minus* of variety
which lowered the sum of the *Friend's* attractions so far
below that of the *Spectator* as to deprive the success of
Addison of all its value as a precedent.

Nor is it easy to agree with the editor of the reprint
of 1837 that the work, "with all its imperfections, is
perhaps the most vigorous " of its author's compositions.
That there are passages in it which impress us by their
force of expression, as well as by subtlety or beauty of
thought, must of course be admitted. It was impossible
to a man of Coleridge's literary power that it should be
otherwise. But "vigorous " is certainly not the adjective
which seems to me to suggest itself to an impartial critic
of these too copious disquisitions. Making every allowance for their necessary elasticity of scope as being

designed to "prepare and discipline the student's moral and intellectual being, not to propound dogmas and theories for his adoption," it must, I think, be allowed that they are wanting in that continuity of movement and co-ordination of parts which, as it seems to me, enters into any intelligible definition of "vigour," as attributed to a work of moral and political exposition considered as a whole. The writer's discursiveness is too often and too vexatiously felt by the reader to permit of the survival of any sense of theorematic unity in his mind; he soon gives up all attempts at periodical measurement of his own and his author's progress towards the prescribed goal of their journey; and he resigns himself in this, as in so many other of Coleridge's prose works, to a study of isolated and detached passages. So treated, however, one may freely admit that the *Friend* is fully worthy of the admiration with which Mr. H. N. Coleridge regarded it. If not the most vigorous, it is beyond all comparison the most characteristic of all his uncle's performances in this field of his multiform activity. In no way could the peculiar pregnancy of Coleridge's thoughts, the more than scholastic subtlety of his dialectic, and the passionate fervour of his spirituality be more impressively exhibited than by a well-made selection of *loci* from the pages of the *Friend*.

CHAPTER VIII.

[1810-1816.]

THE life led by Coleridge during the six years next ensuing is difficult to trace, even in the barest outline; to give a detailed and circumstantial account of it from any ordinarily accessible source of information is impossible. Nor is it, I imagine, very probable that even the most exhaustive search among whatever unprinted records may exist in the possession of his friends would at all completely supply the present lack of biographical material. For not only had it become Coleridge's habit to disappear from the sight of his kinsmen and acquaintances for long periods together; he had fallen almost wholly silent also. They not only ceased to see him, but they ceased to hear of him. Letters addressed to him, even on subjects of the greatest importance, would remain for months unnoticed, and in many instances would receive no answer at all. His correspondence during the next half-dozen years must have been of the

scantiest amount and the most intermittent character,
and a biographer could hope, therefore, for but little aid
in bridging over the large gaps in his knowledge of this
period, even if every extant letter written by Coleridge
during its continuance were to be given to the world.

Such light, too, as is retrospectively thrown upon it by
Coleridge's correspondence of a later date is of the most
fitful description, — scarcely more than serves, in fact,
for the rendering of darkness visible.   Even the sudden
and final departure from the Lakes it leaves involved in
as much obscurity as ever.   Writing to Mr. Thomas
Allsop[1] from Ramsgate twelve years afterwards (8th
October 1822) he says that he "counts four grasping
and griping sorrows in his past life."   The first of these
"was when" [no date given] "the vision of a happy home
sank for ever, and it became impossible for me longer
even to hope for domestic happiness under the name of
husband."   That is plain enough on the whole, though
it still leaves us in some uncertainty as to whether the
"sinking of the vision" was as gradual as the estrangement between husband and wife, or whether he refers
to some violent rupture of relations with Mrs. Coleridge,

---

[1] Coleridge made the acquaintance of this gentleman, who
became his enthusiastic disciple, in 1818.   His chief interest for
us is the fact that for the next seven years he was Coleridge's correspondent.   Personally, he was a man of little judgment or critical
discrimination, and his sense of the ridiculous may be measured
by the following passage.   Speaking of the sweetness of Charles
Lamb's smile, he says that "there is still one man living, a stock-
broker, who has that smile," and adds : "To those who wish to
see the only thing left on earth, *if it is still left*, of Lamb, his best
and most beautiful remain—his smile, I will indicate its possessor,
Mr. —— of Throgmorton Street."   How the original "possessor"
of this apparently assignable security would have longed to "feel
Mr. Allsop's head"!

possibly precipitating his departure from the Lakes.   If
so, the second "griping and grasping sorrow" followed
very quickly on the first, for he says that it overtook
him "on the night of his arrival from Grasmere with
Mr. and Mrs. Montagu;" while in the same breath and
paragraph, and as though undoubtedly referring to the
same thing, he speaks of the "destruction of a friendship of fifteen years when, just at the moment of Fenner
and Curtis's (the publishers) bankruptcy" (by which
Coleridge was a heavy loser, but which did not occur
till seven years afterwards), somebody indicated by
seven asterisks and possessing an income of £1200
a-year, was "totally transformed into baseness."   There
is certainly not much light here, any more than in the
equally enigmatical description of the third sorrow as
being "in some sort included in the second," so that
"what the former was to friendship the latter was to a
still more inward bond."   The truth is, that all Coleridge's references to himself in his later years are
shrouded in a double obscurity.   One veil is thrown
over them by his deliberate preference for abstract and
mystical forms of expression, and another perhaps by
that kind of shameful secretiveness which grows upon
all men who become the slaves of concealed indulgences,
and which often displays itself on occasions when it has
no real object to gain of any kind whatever.

Thus much only we know, that on reaching London
in the summer of 1810 Coleridge became the guest of
the Montagus, and that, after some months' residence
with them, he left as the immediate result of some
difference with his host which was never afterwards
composed.   Whether it arose from the somewhat trivial

cause to which De Quincey has, admittedly upon the
evidence of "the learned in literary scandal," referred
it, it is now impossible to say. But at some time or
other, towards the close probably of 1810, or in the
early months of 1811, Coleridge quitted Mr. Montagu's
house for that of Mr. John Morgan, a companion of his
early Bristol days, and a common friend of his and
Southey's ; and here, at No. 7 Portland Place, Hammer-
smith, he was residing when, for the second time, he
resolved to present himself to the London public in the
capacity of lecturer.   His services were on this occasion
engaged by the London Philosophical Society, at Crane
Court, Fleet Street, and their prospectus announced that
on Monday, 18th November, Mr. Coleridge would com-
mence "a course of lectures on Shakspeare and Milton,
in illustration of the principles of poetry and their application, on grounds of criticism, to the most popular works
of later English poets, those of the living included.
After an introductory lecture on false criticism (especially in poetry) and on its causes, two-thirds of the
remaining course," continues the prospectus, "will be
assigned, 1st, to a philosophical analysis and explanation
of all the principal characters of our great dramatists, as
Othello, Falstaff, Richard the Third, Iago, Hamlet, etc.,
and to a critical comparison of Shakspeare in respect of
diction, imagery, management of the passions, judgment
in the construction of his dramas—in short, of all that
belongs to him as a poet, and as a dramatic poet, with
his contemporaries or immediate successors, Jonson,
Beaumont and Fletcher, Ford, Massinger, and in the
endeavour to determine which of Shakespeare's merits
and defects are common to him, with other writers

of the same age, and what remain peculiar to his genius."

A couple of months before the commencement of this course, viz. in September 1811, Coleridge seems to have entered into a definite journalistic engagement with his old editor, Mr. Daniel Stuart, then the proprietor of the *Courier*. It was not, however, his first connection with that journal. He had already published at least one piece of verse in its columns, and two years before, while the *Friend* was still in existence, he had contributed to it a series of letters on the struggle of the Spaniards against their French invaders. In these, as though to show that under the ashes of his old democratic enthusiasm still lived its wonted fires, and that the inspiration of a popular cause was only needed to reanimate them, we find, with less of the youthful lightness of touch and agility of movement, a very near approach to the vigour of his early journalistic days. Whatever may be thought of the historic value of the parallel which he institutes between the struggle of the Low Countries against their tyrant, and that of the Peninsula against its usurping conqueror, it is worked out with remarkable ingenuity of completeness. Whole pages of the letters are radiant with that steady flame of hatred which, ever since the hour of his disillusionment, had glowed in his breast at the name and thought of Bonaparte ; and whenever he speaks of the Spaniards, of Spanish patriotism, of the Spanish Cortes, we see that the names of "the people," of "freedom," of "popular assembly," have some of their old magic for him still. The following passage is almost pathetic in its reminder of the days of 1792, before that modern Leonidas, the young

French Republic, had degenerated into the Xerxes of the Empire.

" The power which raised up, established, and enriched the Dutch republic,—the same mighty power is no less at work in the present struggle of the Spanish nation, a power which mocks the calculations of ordinary statecraft too subtle to be weighed against it, and mere outward brute force too different from it to admit of comparison.   A power as mighty in the rational creation as the element of electricity in the material world ; and, like that element, infinite in its affinities, infinite in its mode of action, combining the most discordant natures, fixing the most volatile, and arming the sluggish vapour of the marsh with arrows of fire ; working alike in silence and in tempest, in growth and in destruction ; now contracted to an individual soul, and now, as in a moment, dilating itself over a whole nation !   Am I asked what this mighty power may be, and wherein it exists ?   If we are worthy of the fame which we possess as the countrymen of Hampden, Russell, and Algernon Sidney, we shall find the answer in our own hearts.   It is the power of the insulted free-will, steadied by the approving conscience and struggling against brute force and iniquitous compulsion for the common rights of human nature, brought home to our inmost souls by being, at the same time, the rights of our betrayed, insulted, and bleeding country."

And as this passage recalls the most striking characteristics of his earlier style, so may its conclusion serve as a fair specimen of the calmer eloquence of his later manner :—

" It is a painful truth, sir, that these men who appeal most to facts, and pretend to take them for their exclusive guide, are the very persons who most disregard the light of experience when it refers them to the mightiness of their own inner nature, in opposition to those forces which they can see with their eyes, and reduce to figures upon a slate. And yet, sir, what is history for the greater and more useful part but a voice from the sepulchres of our forefathers, assur-

ing us, from *their* united experience, that our spirits are as
much stronger than our bodies as they are nobler and more
permanent ?   The historic muse appears in her loftiest character as the nurse of Hope.   It is her appropriate praise
that her records enable the magnanimous to silence the selfish
and cowardly by appealing to actual *events* for the information of these truths which they themselves first learned from
the surer oracle of their own reason."

But this reanimation of energy was but a transient
phenomenon.   It did not survive the first freshness of
its exciting cause.   The Spanish insurrection grew into
the Peninsular war, and though the glorious series of
Wellington's victories might well, one would think, have
sustained the rhetorical temperature at its proper pitch,
it failed to do so.   Or was it, as the facts appear now
and then to suggest, that Coleridge at Grasmere or
Keswick—Coleridge in the inspiring (and restraining)
companionship of close friends and literary compeers—
was an altogether different man from Coleridge in London,
alone with his thoughts and his opium ?   The question
cannot be answered with confidence, and the fine quality
of the lectures on Shakespeare is sufficient to show that,
for some time, at any rate, after his final migration to
London, his critical faculty retained its full vigour.   But
it is beyond dispute that his regular contributions to
the *Courier* in 1811-12 are not only vastly inferior to his
articles of a dozen years before in the *Morning Post* but
fall sensibly short of the level of the letters of 1809,
from which extract has just been made.   Their tone is
spiritless, and they even lack distinction of style.   Their
very subjects, and the mode of treating them, appear to
show a change in Coleridge's attitude towards public
affairs if not in the very conditions of his journalistic

employment. They have much more of the character
of newspaper hack-work than his earlier contributions.
He seems to have been, in many instances, set to write
a mere report, and often a rather dry and mechanical
report of this or the other Peninsular victory. He
seldom or never discusses the political situation, as his
wont had been, *au large ;* and in place of broad states-
manlike reflection on the scenes and actors in the great
world-drama then in progress, we meet with too much of
that sort of criticism on the consistency and capacity of
"our contemporary, the *Morning Chronicle*," which had
less attraction, it may be suspected, even for the public
of its own day than for the journalistic profession, while
for posterity, of course, it possesses no interest at all. The
series of contributions extends from September of 1811
until April of the following year, and appears to have nearly
come to a premature and abrupt close in the intermediate
July, when an article written by Coleridge in strong
opposition to the proposed reinstatement of the Duke of
York in the command-in-chief was, by ministerial influence, suppressed before publication. This made Coleridge, as his daughter informs us on the authority of
Mr. Crabb Robinson, " very uncomfortable," and he was
desirous of being engaged on another paper. He wished
to be connected with the *Times*, and " I spoke," says
Mr. Robinson, " with Walter on the subject, but the
negotiation failed."

With the conclusion of the lectures on Shakespeare,
and the loss of the stimulus, slight as it then was to him,
of regular duties and recurring engagements, Coleridge
seems to have relapsed once more into thoroughly
desultory habits of work. The series of aphorisms and

reflections which he contributed in 1812 to Southey's *Omniana*, witty, suggestive, profound as many of them are, must not of course be referred to the years in which they were given to the world. They belong unquestionably to the order of *marginalia*, the scattered notes of which De Quincey speaks with not extravagant admiration, and which, under the busy pencil of a commentator always indefatigable in the *strenua inertia* of reading, had no doubt accumulated in considerable quantities over a long course of years.

The disposal, however, of this species of literary material could scarcely have been a source of much profit to him, and Coleridge's difficulties of living must by this time have been growing acute. His pension from the Wedgwoods had been assigned, his surviving son has stated, to the use of his family, and even this had been in the previous year reduced by half. "In Coleridge's neglect," observes Miss Meteyard, "of his duties to his wife, his children, and his friends, must be sought the motives which led Mr. Wedgwood in 1811 to withdraw his share of the annuity. An excellent, even over-anxious father, he was likely to be shocked at a neglect which imposed on the generosity of Southey, himself heavily burdened, those duties which every man of feeling and honour proudly and even jealously guards as his own. . . . The pension of £150 per annum had been originally granted with the view to secure Coleridge independence and leisure while he effected some few of his manifold projects of literary work. But ten years had passed, and these projects were still *in nubibus*—even the life of Lessing, even the briefer memoir of Thomas Wedgwood; and gifts so well intentioned, had as it were,

ministered to evil rather than to good." We can hardly
wonder at the step, however we may regret it; and if
one of the reasons adduced in defence of it savours
somewhat of the fallacy known as *à non causâ pro causâ*,
we may perhaps attribute that rather to the maladroit-
ness of Miss Meteyard's advocacy than to the weakness
of Mr. Wedgwood's logic. The fact, however, that this
"excellent, even over-anxious father" was shocked at a
neglect which imposed a burden on the generosity of
Southey, is hardly a just ground for cutting off one of
the supplies by which that burden was partially relieved.
As to the assignment of the pension to the family, it is
impossible to question what has been positively affirmed
by an actual member of that family, the Rev. Derwent
Coleridge himself; though, when he adds that not only
was the school education of both the sons provided from
this source, but that through his (Coleridge's) influence
they were both sent to college, his statement is at
variance, as will be presently seen, with an authority
equal to his own.

In 1812, at any rate, we may well believe that
Coleridge's necessities had become pressing, and the
timely service then rendered to him by Lord Byron may
have been suggested almost as much by a knowledge of
his needs as by admiration for the dramatic merits of his
long-since rejected tragedy. *Osorio's* time had at any
rate come. The would-be fratricide changed his name
to Ordonio, and ceased to stand sponsor to the play, which
was rechristened *Remorse*, and accepted at last, upon
Byron's recommendation, by the committee of Drury
Lane Theatre, the playhouse at whose doors it had
knocked vainly fifteen years before it was performed

there for the first time on the 23d of January 1813.
The prologue and epilogue, without which in those times
no gentleman's drama was accounted complete, was
written, the former by Charles Lamb, the latter by the
author himself.   It obtained a brilliant success on its
first representation, and was honoured with what was
in those days regarded as the very respectable run of
twenty nights.

The success, however, which came so opportunely for
his material necessities was too late to produce any good
effect upon Coleridge's mental state.   But a month after
the production of his tragedy we find him writing in the
most dismal strain of hypochondria to Thomas Poole.
The only pleasurable sensation which the success of
Remorse had given him was, he declares, the receipt of
his friend's "heart-engendered lines" of congratulation.
"No grocer's apprentice, after his first month's permitted riot, was ever sicker of figs and raisins than I of
hearing about the *Remorse*.   The endless rat-a-tat-tat at
our black-and-blue bruised doors, and my three master-
fiends, proof-sheets, letters, and — worse than these —
invitations to large dinners, which I cannot refuse without offence and imputation of pride, etc., oppress me so
much that my spirits quite sink under it.   I have never
seen the play since the first night.   It has been a good
thing for the theatre.   They will get eight or ten
thousand pounds by it, and I shall get more than by all
my literary labours put together—nay, thrice as much."
So large a sum of money as this must have amounted to
should surely have lasted him for years; but the particular species of intemperance to which he was now
hopelessly enslaved is probably the most costly of all

forms of such indulgence, and it seems pretty evident that the proceeds of his theatrical *coup* were consumed in little more than a year.

Early in 1814, at any rate, Coleridge once more returned to his old occupation of lecturer, and this time not in London, but in the scene of his first appearance in that capacity. The lectures which he proposed to deliver at Bristol were, in fact, a repetition of the course of 1811-12 ; but the ways of the lecturer, to judge from an amusing story recorded by Cottle, more nearly resembled his proceedings in 1808. A "brother of Mr. George Cumberland," who happened to be his fellow-traveller to Bristol on this occasion, relates that before the coach started Coleridge's attention was attracted by a little Jew boy selling pencils, with whom he entered into conversation, and with whose superior qualities he was so impressed as to declare that "if he had not an important engagement at Bristol he would stay behind to provide some better condition for the lad." The coach having started, "the gentleman" (for his name was unknown to the narrator of the incident) "talked incessantly and in a most entertaining way for thirty miles out of London, and, afterwards, with little intermission till they reached Marlborough," when he discovered that a lady in the coach with him was a particular friend of his ; and on arriving at Bath he quitted the coach declaring that he was determined not to leave her till he had seen her safe to her brother's door in North Wales. This was the day fixed for the delivery of Coleridge's first lecture. Two or three days afterwards, having completed his *détour* by North Wales, he arrived at Bristol ; another day was fixed for the commencement of the course, and Coleridge then presented himself an hour after the audience had taken their seats. The "important engagement" might be broken, it seems, for a mere whim, though not for a charitable impulse—a distinction testifying to a mixture of insincerity and unpunctuality not pleasant to note as an evidence of the then state of Coleridge's emotions and will.

Thus inauspiciously commenced, there was no reason why the Bristol lectures of 1814 should be more successful than the London Institution lectures of 1808 ; nor were they, it appears, in fact. They are said to have been "sparsely attended,"—no doubt owing to the natural unwillingness of people to pay for an hour's contemplation of an empty platform ; and their pecuniary returns in consequence were probably insignificant. Coleridge remained in Bristol till the month of August, when he returned to London.

The painful task of tracing his downward course is now almost completed. In the middle of this year he touched the lowest point of his descent. Cottle, who had a good deal of intercourse with him by speech and letter in 1814, and who had not seen him since 1807, was shocked by his extreme prostration, and then for the first time ascertained the cause. "In 1814," he says in his *Recollections*, "S. T. C. had been long, very long, in the habit of taking from two quarts of laudanum a week to a pint a day, and on one occasion he had been known to take in the twenty-four hours a whole quart of laudanum. The serious expenditure of money resulting from this habit was the least evil, though very great, and must have absorbed all the produce of his

writings and lectures and the liberalities of his friends."
Cottle addressed to him a letter of not very delicate
remonstrance on the subject, to which Coleridge replied
in his wontedly humble strain.

There is a certain Pharisaism about the Bristol poet-
publisher which renders it necessary to exercise some
little caution in the acceptance of his account of Coleridge's condition ; but the facts, from whatever source
one seeks them, appear to acquit him of any exaggeration in his summing up of the melancholy matter.   "A
general impression," he says, " prevailed on the minds
of Coleridge's friends that it was a desperate case, that
paralysed all their efforts ; that to assist Coleridge with
money which, under favourable circumstances would
have been most promptly advanced, would now only
enlarge his capacity to obtain the opium which was
consuming him.   We merely knew that Coleridge had
retired with his friend, Mr. John Morgan, to a small
house at Calne in Wiltshire."

It must have been at Calne, then, that Coleridge
composed the series of "Letters to Mr. Justice Fletcher
concerning his charge to the Grand Jury of the county
of Wexford, at the summer Assizes in 1814," which
appeared at intervals in the *Courier* between 20th
September and 10th December of this year.   Their
subject, a somewhat injudiciously animated address to
the aforesaid Grand Jury on the subject of the relations
between Catholicism and Protestantism in Ireland, was
well calculated to stimulate the literary activity of a
man who always took something of the keen interest of
the modern Radical in the eternal Irish question ; and
the letters are not wanting either in argumentative

force or in grave impressiveness of style. But their
lack of spring and energy as compared with Coleridge's
earlier work in journalism is painfully visible throughout.

Calne, it is to be supposed, was still Coleridge's place
of abode when Southey (17th October) wrote Cottle that
letter which appears in his *Correspondence*, and which
illustrates with such sad completeness the contrast
between the careers of the two generous, romantic,
brilliant youths who had wooed their wives together—
and between the fates, one must add, of the two sisters
who had listened to their wooing — eighteen years
before : a letter as honourable to the writer as it is the
reverse to its subject. "Can you," asks Southey, "tell
me anything of Coleridge? A few lines of introduction
for a son of Mr. —— of St. James's, in your city, are
all that we have received from him since I saw him last
September twelvemonth (1813) in town. The children
being thus left entirely to chance, I have applied to his
brothers at Ottey (Ottery?) concerning them, and am in
hopes through their means and the assistance of other
friends of sending Hartley to college. Lady Beaumont
has promised £30 a year for the purpose, and Poole £10.
I wrote to Coleridge three or four months ago, telling
him that unless he took some steps in providing for this
object I must make the application, and required his
answer within a given term of three weeks. He received
the letter, and in his note by Mr. —— promised to
answer it, but he has never taken any further notice of
it. I have acted with the advice of Wordsworth. The
brothers, as I expected, promise their concurrence, and
I daily expect a letter stating to what extent they will
contribute." With this letter before him an impartial

biographer can hardly be expected to adopt the theory
which has commended itself to the filial piety of the
Rev. Derwent Coleridge—namely, that it was through
the father's "influence" that the sons were sent to
college.   On a plain matter of fact such as this, one
may be permitted, without indelicacy, to uphold the con-
clusions compelled by the evidence.   Such expressions of
opinion, on the other hand, as that Coleridge's "separation
from his family, brought about and continued through
the force of circumstances over which he had far
less control than has been commonly supposed, was in
fact nothing else but an ever-prolonged absence;" and
that "from first to last he took an affectionate, it may
be said a passionate, interest in the welfare of his
children"—such expressions of mere opinion as these
it may be proper enough to pass by in respectful
silence.

The following year brought with it no improvement
in the embarrassed circumstances, no reform of the dis-
ordered life.   Still domiciled with Mr. Morgan at Calne,
the self-made sufferer writes to Cottle : "You will wish
to know something of myself.   In health I am not worse
than when at Bristol I was best; yet fluctuating, yet
unhappy, in circumstances poor indeed !   I have collected
my scattered and my manuscript poems sufficient to
make one volume.   Enough I have to make another.
But, till the latter is finished, I cannot, without great
loss of character, publish the former, on account of the
arrangement, besides the necessity of correction.   For
instance, I earnestly wish to begin the volumes with
what has never been seen by any, however few, such as
a series of odes on the different sentences of the Lord's

Prayer, and, more than all this, to finish my greater
work on 'Christianity considered as philosophy, and as
the only philosophy.'" Then follows a request for a
loan of forty pounds on the security of the MSS., an
advance which Cottle declined to make, though he sent
Coleridge "some smaller temporary relief." The letter
concludes with a reference to a project for taking a house
and receiving pupils to board and instruct, which Cottle
appeared to consider the crowning "degradation and
ignominy of all."

A few days later we find Lord Byron again coming to
Coleridge's assistance with a loan of a hundred pounds
and words of counsel and encouragement. Why should
not the author of *Remorse* repeat his success? "In
Kean," writes Byron, "there is an actor worthy of ex-
pressing the thoughts of the character which you have
every power of embodying, and I cannot but regret that
the part of Ordonio was disposed of before his appearance at Drury Lane. We have had nothing to be mentioned in the same breath with *Remorse* for very many
years, and I should think that the reception of that play
was sufficient to encourage the highest hopes of author
and audience." The advice was followed, and the drama
of *Zapolya* was the result. It is a work of even less
dramatic strength than its predecessor, and could scarcely,
one thinks, have been as successful with an audience.
It was not, however, destined to see the footlights.
Before it had passed the tribunal of the Drury Lane
Committee it had lost the benefit of Byron's patronage
through the poet's departure from England, and the
play was rejected by Mr. Douglas Kinnaird, the then
reader for the theatre, who assigned, according to

Mr. Gillman, "some ludicrous objections to the meta-physics." Before leaving England, however, Byron rendered a last, and, as the result proved, a not unimportant service to his brother-poet. He introduced him to Mr. Murray, who, in the following year, undertook the publication of *Christabel*—the most successful, in the sense of the most popular, of all its author's productions in verse.

With the coming of spring in the following year that dreary story of slow self-destruction, into which the narrative of Coleridge's life from the age of thirty to that of forty-five resolves itself, was brought to a close. Coleridge had at last perceived that his only hope of redemption lay in a voluntary submission of his enfeebled will to the control of others, and he had apparently just enough strength of volition to form and execute the necessary resolve. He appears, in the first instance, to have consulted a physician of the name of Adams, who, on the 9th of April 1816, put himself in communication with Mr. Gillman of Highgate. "A very learned, but in one respect an unfortunate gentleman, has," he wrote, "applied to me on a singular occasion. He has for several years been in the habit of taking large quantities of opium. For some time past he has been in vain endeavouring to break himself of it. It is apprehended his friends are not firm enough, from a dread lest he should suffer by suddenly leaving it off, though he is conscious of the contrary, and has proposed to me to submit himself to any regimen, however severe. With this view he wishes to fix himself in the house of some medical gentleman who will have the courage to refuse him any laudanum, and under whose assistance, should

he be the worse for it, he may be relieved." Would
such a proposal, inquires the writer, be absolutely
inconsistent with Mr. Gillman's family arrangements?
He would not, he adds, have proposed it "but on account of the great importance of the character as a
literary man. His communicative temper will make his
society very interesting as well as useful." Mr. Gillman's acquaintance with Dr. Adams was but slight, and
he had had no previous intention of receiving an inmate
into his house. But the case very naturally interested
him; he sought an interview with Dr. Adams, and it
was agreed that the latter should drive Coleridge to
Highgate the following evening. At the appointed
hour, however, Coleridge presented himself alone, and,
after spending the evening at Mr. Gillman's, left him,
as even in his then condition he left most people who
met him for the first time, completely captivated by the
amiability of his manners and the charm of his conversation. The next day Mr. Gillman received from him a
letter, finally settling the arrangement to place himself
under the doctor's care, and concluding with the following pathetic passage :—

"And now of myself. My ever wakeful reason and the
keenness of my moral feelings will secure you from all
unpleasant circumstances connected with me save only one,
viz. the evasion of a specific madness. You will never *hear*
anything but truth from me ; prior habits render it out of my
power to tell an untruth, but, unless carefully observed, I
dare not promise that I should not, with regard to this de-
tested poison, be capable of acting one. Not sixty hours
have yet passed without my having taken laudanum, though,
for the last week, comparatively trifling doses. I have full
belief that your anxiety need not be extended beyond the
first week, and for the first week, I shall not, must not, be

permitted to leave your house, unless with you ; delicately or indelicately, this must be done, and both the servants, and the assistant, must receive absolute commands from you. The stimulus of conversation suspends the terror that haunts my mind ; but, when I am alone, the horrors I have suffered from laudanum, the degradation, the blighted utility, almost overwhelm me. If (as I feel for the *first time* a soothing confidence that it will prove) I should leave you restored to my moral and bodily health, it is not myself only that will love and honour you ; every friend I have (and, thank God ! in spite of this wretched vice I have many and warm ones, who were friends of my youth, and have never deserted me) will thank you with reverence. I have taken no notice of your kind apologies. If I could not be comfortable in your house and with your family, I should deserve to be miserable."

This letter was written on a Saturday, and on the following Monday Coleridge presented himself at Mr. Gillman's, bringing in his hand the proof - sheets of *Christabel*, now printed for the first time. He had looked, as the letter just quoted shows, with a " soothing confidence " to leaving his retreat at some future period in a restored condition of moral and bodily health ; and as regards the restoration, his confidence was in a great measure justified. But the friendly doors which opened to receive him on this 15th of April 1816, were destined to close only upon his departing bier. Under the watchful and almost reverential care of this well - chosen guardian, sixteen years of comparatively quiet and well-ordered life, of moderate but effective literary activity, and of gradual though never complete emancipation from his fatal habit, were reserved to him. He had still, as we shall see, to undergo certain recurrences of restlessness and renewals of pecuniary difficulty ; his shattered health was but imperfectly and temporarily

repaired; his "shaping spirit of imagination" could
not and did not return; his transcendental brood-
ings became more and more the "habit of his soul."
But henceforth he recovers for us a certain measure of
his long-lost dignity, and a figure which should always
have been "meet for the reverence of the hearth" in the
great household of English literature, but which had
far too long and too deeply sunk below it, becomes once
more a worthy and even a venerable presence. At
evening-time it was light.

CHAPTER IX.

Life at Highgate—Renewed activity—Publications and re-
publications—The *Biographia Literaria*—The lectures
of 1818—Coleridge as a Shakespearian critic.

[1816-1818.]

THE results of the step which Coleridge had just taken
became speedily visible in more ways than one, and the
public were among the first to derive benefit from it.
For not only was he stimulated to greater activity of
production, but his now more methodical way of life
gave him time and inclination for that work of arrangement and preparation for the press which, distasteful
to most writers, was no doubt especially irksome to
him, and thus insured the publication of many pieces
which otherwise might never have seen the light. The
appearance of *Christabel* was, as we have said, received
with signal marks of popular favour, three editions
being called for and exhausted in the same year. In
1816 there appeared also *The Statesman's Manual ; or
the Bible the best guide to Political Skill and Foresight :
a Lay Sermon addressed to the higher classes of Society,
with an Appendix containing Comments and Essays connected with the Study of the Inspired Writings ;* in 1817,

another *Lay Sermon addressed to the higher and middle
classes on the existing distresses and discontents;* and in
the same year followed the most important publication
of this period, the *Biographia Literaria.*

In 1817, too, it was that Coleridge at last made his
long-meditated collection and classification of his already
published poems, and that for the first time something
approaching to a complete edition of the poet's works
was given to the world. The *Sibylline Leaves,* as this
reissue was called, had been intended to be preceded by
another volume of verse, and "accordingly on the
printer's signatures of every sheet we find Vol. II.
appearing." Too characteristically, however, the scheme
was abandoned, and Volume II. emerged from the press
without any Volume I. to accompany it. The drama
of *Zapolya* followed in the same year, and proved more
successful with the public than with the critic of Drury
Lane. The "general reader" assigned no "ludicrous
objections to its metaphysics;" on the contrary, he took
them on trust, as his generous manner is, and *Zapolya,*
published thus as a Christmas tale, became so immediately popular that two thousand copies were sold in
six weeks. In the year 1818 followed the three-volume
selection of essays from the *Friend,* a reissue to which
reference has already been made. With the exception
of *Christabel,* however, all the publications of these three
years unfortunately proceeded from the house of Gale
and Fenner, a firm which shortly afterwards became
bankrupt; and Coleridge thus lost all or nearly all of the
profits of their sale.

The most important of the new works of this period
was, as has been said, the *Biographia Literaria,* or, to give

it its other title, *Biographical Sketches of my Literary Life
and Opinions.* Its interest, however, is wholly critical and
illustrative; as a narrative it would be found extremely
disappointing and probably irritating by the average
reader. With the exception of one or two incidental
disclosures, but little biographical information is to be
derived from it which is not equally accessible from
sources independent of the author; and the almost complete want of sequence and arrangement renders it a very
inconvenient work of reference even for these few biographical details. Its main value is to be found in the
contents of seven chapters, from the fourteenth to the
twentieth; but it is not going too far to say that, in
respect of these, it is literally priceless. No such
analysis of the principles of poetry—no such exact discrimination of what was sound in the modern "return-to-
nature" movement from what was false—has ever been
accomplished by any other critic, or with such admirable
completeness by this consummate critic at any other
time. Undoubtedly it is not of the light order of reading; none, or very little, of Coleridge's prose is. The
whole of chapter xv., for instance, in which the specific
elements of "poetic power" are "distinguished from
general talent determined to poetic composition by accidental motives," requires a close and sustained effort of the
attention, but those who bestow it will find it amply repaid. I know of no dissertation conceived and carried out
in terms of the abstract which in the result so triumphantly justifies itself upon application to concrete cases.
As regards the question of poetic *expression*, and the laws
by which its true form is determined, Coleridge's analysis
is, it seems to me, final. I cannot, at least, after the most

careful reflection upon it, conceive it as being other than
the absolutely last word on the subject. Reasoning and
illustration are alike so convincing that the reader, like
the contentious student who listened unwillingly to his
professor's demonstration of the first proposition of
Euclid, is compelled to confess that "he has nothing to
reply." To the judicious admirer of Wordsworth, to
every one who, while recognising Wordsworth's inestim-
able services to English literature as the leader of the
naturalist reaction in poetry, has yet been vaguely
conscious of the defect in his poetic theory, and very
keenly conscious of the vices of his poetic practice,—to
all such persons it must be a profound relief and satisfaction to be guided as unerringly as Coleridge guides
them to the "parting of the ways" of truth and falsity
in Wordsworth's doctrines, and to be enabled to perceive
that nothing which has offended him in that poet's
thought and diction has any real connection with whatever in the poet's principles has commanded his assent.
There is no one who has ever felt uneasy under the
blasphemies of the enemy but must entertain deep
gratitude for so complete a discharge as Coleridge has
procured him from the task of defending such lines as—

> "And I have travelled far as Hull to see
> What clothes he might have left or other property."

Defend them indeed the ordinary reader probably would
not, preferring even the abandonment of his theory to
a task so humiliating. But the theory has so much of
truth and value in it that the critic who has redeemed it
from the discredit of Wordsworth's misapplications of it
is entitled to the thanks of every friend of simplicity,

who is at the same time an enemy of bathos. There
is no longer any reason to treat the deadly common-
places, amid which we toil through so many pages of the
Excursion, as having any true theoretic affinity with its
but too occasional majestic interludes. The smooth
square-cut blocks of prose which insult the natural
beauty of poetic rock and boulder even in such a scene
of naked moorland grandeur as that of *Resolution and
Independence* are seen and shown to be the mere in-
truders which we have all felt them to be. To the
Wordsworthian, anxious for a full justification of the
faith that is in him, the whole body of Coleridge's
criticism on his friend's poetry in the *Biographia Literaria*
may be confidently recommended. The refutation of
what is untenable in Wordsworth's theory, the censure
pronounced upon certain characteristics of his practice,
are made all the more impressive by the tone of cordial
admiration which distinguishes every personal reference
to the poet himself, and by the unfailing discrimination
with which the critic singles out the peculiar beauties of
his poetry. No finer selection of finely characteristic
Wordsworthian passages could perhaps have been made
than those which Coleridge has quoted in illustration
of his criticisms in the eighteenth and two following
chapters of the *Biographia Literaria.* For the rest,
however, unless indeed one excepts the four chapters on the Hartleian system and its relation to the
German school of philosophy, the book is rather one
to be dipped into for the peculiar pleasure which an
hour in Coleridge's company must always give to
any active intelligence, than to be systematically studied
with a view to perfecting one's conception of Cole-

ridge's philosophical and critical genius considered in
its totality.

As to the two lay sermons, the less ambitious of them
is decidedly the more successful. The advice to "the
higher and middle classes" on the existing distresses and
discontents contains at least an ingredient of the practical;
its distinctively religious appeals are varied by sound
political and economical arguments; and the enumeration
and exposure of the various artifices by which most
orators are accustomed to delude their hearers is as
masterly as only Coleridge could have made it. Who
but he, for instance, could have thrown a piece of subtle
observation into a form in which reason and fancy unite
so happily to impress it on the mind as in the following
passage : "The mere appeal to the auditors, whether the
arguments are not such that none but an idiot or an
hireling could resist, is an effective substitute for any
argument at all. For mobs have no memories. They
are in nearly the same state as that of an individual
when he makes what is termed a bull. *The passions, like
a fused metal, fill up the wide interstices of thought and supply
the defective links; and thus incompatible assertions are
harmonised by the sensation, without the sense of connection.*"
The other lay sermon, however, the *Statesman's Manual*,
is less appropriately conceived. Its originating proposition, that the Bible is "the best guide to political skill
and foresight," is undoubtedly open to dispute, but
might nevertheless be capable of plausible defence upon
à *priori* grounds. Coleridge, however, is not content
with this method of procedure; as, indeed, with so
avowedly practical an object in view he scarcely could
be, for a "manual" is essentially a work intended for

the constant consultation of the artificer in the actual performance of his work, and ought at least to contain illustrations of the application of its general principles to particular cases.   It is in undertaking to supply these that the essential mysticism of Coleridge's counsels comes to light.   For instance : "I am deceived if you will not be compelled to admit that the prophet Isaiah revealed the true philosophy of the French Revolution more than two thousand years before it became a sad irrevocable truth of history.   'And thou saidst, I shall be a lady for ever, so that thou didst not lay these things to thy heart neither didst remember the latter end of it. . . .   Therefore shall evil come upon thee ; thou shalt not know from whence it riseth, etc.' "   And to this last-quoted sentence Coleridge actually appends the following note : "The reader will scarcely fail to find in this verse a remembrancer of the sudden setting in of the frost before the usual time (in a country, too, where the commencement of its two seasons is in general scarcely less regular than that of the wet and dry seasons between the tropics) which caused, and the desolation which accompanied, the flight from Moscow."   One can make no other comment upon this than that if it really be wisdom which statesmen would do well to lay to heart, the late Dr. Cumming must have been the most profound instructor in statesmanship that the world has ever seen. A prime minister of real life, however, could scarcely be seriously recommended to shape his policy upon a due consideration of the possible allegoric meaning of a passage in Isaiah, to say nothing of the obvious objection that this kind of appeal to *Sortes Biblicæ* is dangerously liable to be turned against those who recommend it.

On the whole, one must say of this lay sermon that it
justifies the apprehension expressed by the author in its
concluding pages.   It does rather "resemble the over-
flow of an earnest mind than an orderly and premedi-
tated," in the sense, at any rate, of a well-considered
"composition."

In the month of January 1818 Coleridge once more
commenced the delivery of a course of lectures in
London. The scope of this series—fourteen in number—
was, as will be seen from the subjoined syllabus, an
immensely comprehensive one.   The subject of the first
was "the manners, morals, literature, philosophy, religion,
and state of society in general in European Christendom,
from the eighth to the fifteenth century;" and of the
second "the tales and metrical romances common for
the most part to England, Germany, and the north of
France; and English songs and ballads continued to the
reign of Charles I."   In the third the lecturer proposed
to deal with the poetry of Chaucer and Spenser, of
Petrarch, and of Ariosto, Pulci, and Boiardo. The fourth,
fifth, and sixth were to be devoted to the dramatic
works of Shakespeare, and to comprise the substance of
Coleridge's former courses on the same subject, "enlarged
and varied by subsequent study and reflection."   In the
seventh he was to treat of the other principal dramatists
of the Elizabethan period, Ben Jonson, Massinger, and
Beaumont and Fletcher; in the eighth of the life and
all the works of Cervantes; in the ninth of Rabelais,
Swift, and Sterne, with a dissertation "on the nature
and constituents of genuine humour, and on the distinctions of humorous from the witty, the fanciful, the
droll, the odd, etc."   Donne, Dante, and Milton formed

the subject of the tenth; the *Arabian Nights Entertainment*, and the *romantic* use of the supernatural in poetry, that of the eleventh. The twelfth was to be on "tales of witches and apparitions, etc.," as distinguished from magic and magicians of Asiatic origin; and the thirteenth, "on colour, sound, and form in nature, as connected with Poesy—the word 'Poesy' being used as the *generic* or class term including poetry, music, painting, statuary, and ideal architecture as its species, the reciprocal relations of poetry and philosophy to each other, and of both to religion and the moral sense." In the fourteenth and final lecture Coleridge proposed to discuss "the corruptions of the English language since the reign of Queen Anne, in our style of writing prose," and to formulate "a few easy rules for the attainment of a manly, unaffected, and pure language in our genuine mother tongue, whether for the purposes of writing, oratory, or conversation."

These lectures, says Mr. Gillman, were from Coleridge's own account more profitable than any he had before given, though delivered in an unfavourable situation; a lecture-room in Flower de Luce Court, which, however, being near the Temple, secured to him the benefit—if benefit it were—of a considerable number of law students among his auditors. It was the first time that his devoted guardian had ever heard him in public, and he reports the significant fact that though Coleridge lectured from notes, which he had carefully made, "it was obvious that his audience were more delighted when, putting his notes aside, he spoke extempore. . . ." He was brilliant, fluent, and rapid; his words seemed to flow as from a person repeating with grace and energy

M

some delightful poem.   If he sometimes paused, it was
not for the want of words, but that he was seeking their
most appropriate or most logical arrangement.

An incident related with extreme, though in a great
measure unconscious, drollery by Mr. Gillman in connection with a lecture delivered at this period is to my
mind of more assistance than many of the accounts of
his "lay sermons" in private circles, in enabling us to
comprehend one element of Coleridge's marvellous
powers of discourse.   Early one morning at Mr. Gillman's
he received two letters—one to inform him that he was
expected that same evening to deliver a lecture, at the
rooms of the London Philosophical Society, to an audience of some four or five hundred persons ; the other
containing a list of the previous lecturers and the lectures
delivered by them during the course of the season.   At
seven o'clock in the evening Coleridge and Mr. Gillman
went up to town to make some inquiries respecting this
unexpected application ; but, on arriving at the house of
the gentleman who had written the letter, they were
informed that he was not at home, but would return at
eight o'clock—the hour fixed for the commencement of
the lecture.   They then proceeded to the Society's rooms,
where in due time the audience assembled ; and the committee having at last entered and taken their places on
the seats reserved for them, " Mr. President arose from
the centre of the group, and, putting on a 'president's hat,'
which so disfigured him that we could scarcely refrain
from laughter, addressed the company in these words :
This evening Mr. Coleridge will deliver a lecture on
' the Growth of the Individual Mind.' "   Coleridge at
first " seemed startled," as well he might, and turning

round to Mr. Gillman whispered : "A pretty stiff subject they have chosen for me." However, he instantly mounted his standing-place and began without hesitation, previously requesting his friend to observe the effect of his lecture on the audience. It was agreed that, should he appear to fail, Gillman was to "clasp his ancle; but that he was to continue for an hour if the countenances of his auditors indicated satisfaction." Coleridge then began his address in these words : "The lecture I am about to give this evening is purely extempore. Should you find a nominative case looking out for a verb, or a fatherless verb for a nominative case, you must excuse it. It is purely extempore, though I have read and thought much on the subject." At this the company smiled, which seemed to inspire the lecturer with confidence. He plunged at once into his lecture—and most brilliant, eloquent, and logically consecutive it was. The time moved on so swiftly that Mr. Gillman found, on looking at his watch, that an hour and a half had passed away, and, therefore, he continues "waiting only a desirable moment—to use his own playful words—I prepared myself to punctuate his oration. As previously agreed, I pressed his ancle, and thus gave him the hint he had requested; when, bowing graciously, and with a benevolent and smiling countenance, he presently descended. The lecture was quite new to me, and I believe quite new to himself so far as the arrangement of his words was concerned. The floating thoughts were beautifully arranged, and delivered on the spur of the moment. What accident gave rise to the singular request, that he should deliver this lecture impromptu, I never learnt; nor did it signify, as it afforded a happy opportunity to

many of witnessing in part the extent of his reading and
the extraordinary strength of his powers."

It is tantalising to think that no record of this remarkable performance remains; but, indeed, the same
may to some extent be said, and in various degrees, of
nearly all the lectures which Coleridge ever delivered.
With the exception of seven out of the fifteen of 1811,
which were published in 1856 by Mr. Payne Collier from
shorthand notes taken at the time, Coleridge's lectures
scarcely exist for us otherwise than in the form of rough
preparatory notes. A few longer pieces, such as the
admirable observations in the second volume of the
Literary Remains, on poetry, on the Greek drama, and on
the progress of the dramatic art in England, are, with
the exception above noticed, almost the only general
disquisitions on these subjects which appear to have
reached us in a complete state. Of the remaining contents of the volume, including the detailed criticisms—
now textual, now analytic—of the various plays of Shakespeare, a considerable portion is frankly fragmentary,
pretending, indeed, to no other character than that of
mere *marginalia*. This, however, does not destroy—I
had almost said it does not even impair—their value.
It does but render them all the more typical productions
of a writer, whose greatest services to mankind in almost
every department of human thought and knowledge with
which he concerned himself were much the most often
performed in the least methodical way. In reading
through these incomparable notes on Shakespeare we soon
cease to lament, or even to remember, their unconnected
form and often somewhat desultory appearance; if, indeed, we do not see reason to congratulate ourselves that

the annotator, unfettered by the restraints which the composition of a systematic treatise would have imposed upon him, is free to range with us at will over many a flower-strewn field, for which otherwise he could not perhaps have afforded to quit the main road of his subject. And this liberty is the more welcome, because Coleridge, *primus inter pares* as a critic of any order of literature, is in the domain of Shakespearian commentary absolute king. The principles of analysis which he was charged with having borrowed without acknowledgment from Schlegel, with whose Shakespearian theories he was at the time entirely unacquainted, were in fact of his own excogitation. He owed nothing in this matter to any individual German, nor had he anything in common with German Shakespearianism except its profoundly philosophising spirit, which, moreover, was in his case directed and restrained by other qualities, too often wanting in critics of that industrious race ; for he possessed a sense of the ridiculous, a feeling for the poetic, a tact, a taste, and a judgment, which would have saved many a worthy but heavy-handed Teutonic professor, who should have been lucky enough to own these gifts, from exposing himself and his science to the satire of the light-minded. Very rarely, indeed, do we find Coleridge indulging *plus æquo* his passion for psychological analysis. Deeply as his criticism penetrates, it is yet loyally recognitive of the opacity of milestones. Far as he sees into his subject, we never find him fancying that he sees beyond the point at which the faculty of human vision is exhausted. His conception of the more complex of Shakespeare's personages, his theory of their characters, his reading of their motives, is often subtle, but always sane; his interpretation of the master's own dealings with them, and of the language which he puts into their mouths, is often highly imaginative, but it is rarely fanciful. Take, as an illustration of the first-mentioned merit, the following acute but eminently sensible estimate of the character of Polonius :—

"He is the personified memory of wisdom no longer actually possessed. This admirable character is always misrepresented on the stage. Shakspeare never intended to exhibit him as a buffoon; for although it was natural for Hamlet—a young man of fire and genius, detesting formality and disliking Polonius on political grounds, as imagining that he had assisted his uncle in his usurpation—should express himself satirically, yet this must not be taken exactly as the poet's conception of him. In Polonius a certain induration of character had arisen from long habits of business; but take his advice to Laertes, and Ophelia's reverence for his memory, and we shall see that he was meant to be represented as a statesman somewhat past his faculties—his recollections of life all full of wisdom, and showing a knowledge of human nature, while what immediately takes place before him and escapes from him is indicative of weakness."

Or this comment on the somewhat faint individualisation of the figure of Lear :—

"In Lear old age is itself a character—natural imperfections being increased by life-long habits of receiving a prompt obedience. Any addition of individualisation would have been unnecessary and painful; for the relation of others to him, of wondrous fidelity and of frightful ingratitude, alone sufficiently distinguish him. Thus Lear becomes the open and ample playroom of nature's passions."

Or lastly, in illustration of my second point, let us take this note on the remark of the knight that "since my young lady's going into France the fool hath much pined away " :—

" The fool is no comic buffoon to make the groundlings laugh—no forced condescension of Shakspeare's genius to the taste of his audience.   Accordingly the poet prepares us for the introduction, which he never does with any of his common clowns and fools, by bringing him into living connection with the pathos of the play.   He is as wonderful a creation as Caliban,—his wild babblings and inspired idiocy articulate. and gauge the horrors of the scene."

The subject is a tempting one to linger over, did not imperative exigencies of space compel me to pass on from it.   There is much—very much—more critical matter in the *Literary Remains* of which it is hard to forbear quotation; and I may mention in particular the profoundly suggestive remarks on the nature of the humorous, with their accompanying analysis of the genius and artistic method of Sterne.   But it is, as has been said, in Shakespearian criticism that Coleridge's unique mastery of all the tools of the critic is most conspicuous, and it is in the brilliant, if unmethodised, pages which I have been discussing that we may most readily find consolation for the too early silencing of his muse.   For these consummate criticisms are essentially and above all the criticisms of a poet.   They are such as could not have been achieved by any man not originally endowed with that divine gift which was fated in this instance to expend itself within so few years.   Nothing, indeed, could more strikingly illustrate the commanding advantage possessed by a poet interpreting a poet than is to be found in Coleridge's occasional sarcastic comments on the *banalités* of our national poet's most prosaic commentator, Warburton—the "thought-swarming, but idealess Warburton," as he once felicitously styles him. The one man seems to read his author's text under the clear, diffused, unwavering radiance emitted from his own poetic imagination; while the criticism of the other resembles a perpetual scratching of damp matches, which flash a momentary light into one corner of the dark passage, and then go out.

CHAPTER X.

Closing years—Temporary renewal of money troubles—The
Aids to Reflection—Growing weakness—Visit to Germany with the Wordsworths—Last illness and death.

[1818-1834.]

FOR the years which now remained to Coleridge, some
sixteen in number, dating from his last appearance as
a public lecturer, his life would seem to have been attended with something, at least, of that sort of happiness
which is enjoyed by the nation of uneventful annals.
There is little to be told of him in the way of literary
performance ; little record remains, unfortunately, of the
discursively didactic talk in which, during these years, his
intellectual activity found its busiest exercise ; of incident
in the ordinary sense of the word there is almost none.
An account of these closing days of his life must resolve
itself almost wholly into a "history of opinion,"—an
attempt to reanimate for ourselves that life of perpetual
meditation which Coleridge lived, and to trace, so far as
the scanty evidence of his utterances enables us to do
so, the general tenor of his daily thoughts. From one
point of view, of course, this task would be extremely
difficult, if not impossible ; from another comparatively

easy.   It is easy, that is to say, to investigate Coleridge's
speculations, so far as their subject is concerned, whatever difficulties their obscurity and subtlety may present
to the inquirer; for, as a matter of fact, their subject is
remarkably uniform.   Attempts to divide the literary
life of a writer into eras are more often arbitrary and
fanciful than not; but the peculiar circumstances of
Coleridge's career did in fact effect the division for
themselves.   His life until the age of twenty-six may
fairly be described as in its "poetic period."   It was
during these years, and indeed during the last two or
three of them, that he produced all the poetry by which
he will be remembered, while he produced little else of
mark or memorability.   The twenty years which follow
from 1798 to 1818 may with equal accuracy be styled
the "critical period."   It was during these years that he
did his best work as a journalist, and all his work as a
public lecturer on æsthetics.   It was during them that he
said his say, and even his final say, so far as any public
modes of expression were concerned, on politics and on
art.   From 1818 to his death his life was devoted
entirely to metaphysics and theology, and with such
close and constant reference to the latter subject, to
which indeed his metaphysics had throughout his life
been ancillary, that it deserves to give the name of the
"theological period" to these closing years.

Their lack of incident, however, is not entirely as
favourable a circumstance as that uneventfulness of
national annals to which I have compared it; for,
though "no news may be good news" in the case of a
nation's history, it is by no means as certainly so in the
case of a man's biography, and, least of all, when the sub-

ject is a man whose inward life of thought and feeling
so completely overshadowed his outward life of action
throughout his whole career.   There is indeed evidence,
slight in amount, but conclusive in character—plain and
painful evidence enough to show that at least the first
four or five years of the period we have mentioned were
not altogether years of resignation and calm ; that they
were embittered by recurring agonies of self-reproach, by

> " Sense of past youth, and manhood come in vain,
>   And genius given, and knowledge won in vain ; "

and by the desolating thought that all which had been
"culled in wood-walks wild," and " all which patient toil
had reared," were to be

> —" but flowers
> Strewn on the corse, and borne upon the bier,
> In the same coffin, for the self-same grave ! "

Here and there in the correspondence with Thomas
Allsop we obtain a glimpse into that vast half-darkened
arena in which this captive spirit self-condemned to the
lions was struggling its last.   To one strange and hitherto unexplained letter I have already referred.   It was
written from Ramsgate in the autumn of 1822, evidently
under circumstances of deep depression.   But there is a
letter nearly two years earlier in date addressed to the
same correspondent which contains by far the fullest
account of Coleridge's then condition of mind, the
state of his literary engagements and his literary
projects, his completed and uncompleted work.   As
usual with him it is stress of money matters that
prompts him to write, and he prefaces his request for
assistance with the following portentous catalogue of

realised or contemplated schemes. "Contemplated," indeed, is too modest a word, according to his own account,
to be applied to any one item in the formidable list.   Of
all of them, he has, he tells Allsop, "already the *written*
materials and contents, requiring only to be put together
from the loose papers and commonplace in memorandum
books, and needing no other change, whether of omission,
addition, or correction, than the mere act of arranging,
and the opportunity of seeing the whole collectively,
bring with them of course."   Heads I. and II. of the list
comprise those criticisms on Shakespeare and the other
principal Elizabethan dramatists; on Dante, Spenser,
Milton, Cervantes, Calderon; on Chaucer, Ariosto, Donne,
Rabelais, etc., which formed the staple of the course of
lectures delivered in 1818, and which were published after
his death in the first two of the four volumes of *Literary
Remains* brought out under the editorship of Mr. H. N.
Coleridge.   Reserving No. III. for a moment we find No.
IV. to consist of "Letters on the Old and New Testament,
and on the Doctrines and Principles held in common by
the Fathers and Founders of the Reformation, addressed
to a Candidate for Holy Orders, including advice on the
plan and subjects of preaching proper to a minister of
the Established Church."   The letters never apparently
saw the light of publicity, at any rate, in the epistolary
form, either during the author's lifetime or after his
death; and with regard to II. and III., which did obtain
posthumous publication, the following caution should
be borne in mind by the reader.   "To the completion,"
says Coleridge, "of these four works I have literally
nothing more to do than to transcribe; but, as I before
hinted, from so many scraps and Sibylline leaves, includ-

ing margins of blank pages that unfortunately I must be my own scribe, and, not done by myself, they will be all but lost." As matters turned out he was not his own scribe, and the difficulty which Mr. Nelson Coleridge experienced in piecing together the fragmentary materials at his disposal is feelingly described by him in his preface to the first edition. He added that the contents of these volumes were drawn from a portion only of the MSS. entrusted to him, and that the remainder of the collection, which, under favourable circumstances, he hoped might hereafter see the light, "was at least of equal value" with what he was then presenting to the reader. This hope was never realised; and it must be remembered, therefore, that the published record of Coleridge's achievements as a critic is, as has already been pointed out, extremely imperfect.[1] That it is not even more disappointingly so than it is, may well entitle his nephew and editor to the gratitude of posterity; but where much has been done, there yet remains much to do ere Coleridge's consummate analyses of poetic and dramatic works can be presented to the reader in other than their present shape of a series of detached brilliancies. The pearls are there, but the string is wanting. Whether it will be ever supplied, or whether it is possible now to supply it, one cannot say.

The third of Coleridge's virtually completed works— there is much virtue in a "virtually"—was a " History of Philosophy considered as a Tendency of the Human

---

[1] How imperfect, a comparison between estimated and actual bulk will show. No. I. was, according to Coleridge's reckoning, to form three volumes of 500 pages each. In the *Literary Remains* it fills less than half of four volumes of little more than 400 pages each.

Mind to exhibit the Powers of the Human Reason, to
discover by its own strength the Origin and Laws of Man
and the World, from Pythagoras to Locke and Condillac."
This production, however, considerable as it is, was probably merely ancillary to what he calls "My GREAT
WORK, to the preparation of which more than twenty
years of my life have been devoted, and on which my
hopes of extensive and permanent utility, of fame in
the noblest sense of the word, mainly rest." To this work
he goes on to say :—

> "All my other writings, unless I except my Poems (and
> these I can exclude in part only), are introductory and pre-
> parative, while its result, if the premises be as I with the
> most tranquil assurance am convinced they are—incontrovert-
> ible, the deductions legitimate, and the conclusions commensu-
> rate, and only commensurate with both [must be], to effect a
> revolution in all that has been called Philosophy and Meta-
> physics in England and France since the era of commencing
> predominance of the mechanical system at the Restoration
> of our Second Charles, and with [in] the present fashionable
> views not only of religion, morals, and politics, but even of
> the modern physics and physiology."

This, it must be allowed, is a sufficiently "large
order," being apparently indeed nothing less than an
undertaking to demolish the system of Locke and his
successors, and to erect German Transcendentalism on
the ruins. With anything less than this, however—
with any less noble object or less faith in their attainments—Coleridge could not, he declares, have stood
acquitted of folly and abuse of time, talent, and learning,
on a labour of three-fourths of his intellectual life.
Somewhat more than a volume of this *magnum opus* had
been dictated by him to his "friend and enlightened

pupil, Mr. Green, so as to exist fit for the press ; " and more than as much again had been done, but he had been compelled to break off the weekly meetings with his pupil from the necessity of writing on subjects of the passing day. Then comes a reference, the last we meet with, to the real "great work," as the unphilo-sophic world has always considered and will always consider it. On this subject he says :—

"Of my poetic works I would fain finish the *Christabel.* Alas ! for the proud time when I planned, when I had present to my mind the materials as well as the scheme of the Hymns entitled Spirit, Sun, Earth, Air, Water, Fire, and Man ; and the Epic Poem on what appears to me the only fit subject remaining for an Epic Poem—Jerusalem besieged and destroyed by Titus."

And then there follows this most pathetic passage, necessary, in spite of its length, to be transcribed entire, both on account of the value of its biographic details—its information on the subject of the useless worldly affairs, etc.—and because of the singularly penetrating light which it throws upon the mental and moral nature of the man :—

"I have only by fits and starts ever prayed—I have not prevailed upon myself to pray to God in sincerity and entire-ness for the fortitude that might enable me to resign myself to the abandonment of all my life's best hopes, to say boldly to myself, 'Gifted with powers confessedly above mediocrity, aided by an education of which no less from almost un-exampled hardships and sufferings than from manifold and peculiar advantages I have never yet found a parallel, I have devoted myself to a life of unintermitted reading, thinking, meditating, and observing, I have not only sacri-ficed all worldly prospects of wealth and advancement, but have in my inmost soul stood aloof from temporary reputation. In consequence of these toils and this self-dedication I possess a calm and clear consciousness that in many and most important departments of truth and beauty I have out-strode my contemporaries, those at least of highest name, that the number of my printed works bear witness that I have not been idle, and the seldom acknowledged but strictly *proveable* effects of my labours appropriated to the welfare of my age in the *Morning Post* before the peace of Amiens, in the *Courier* afterwards, and in the serious and various subjects of my lectures . . . (add to which the unlimited freedom of my communications to colloquial life) may surely be allowed as evidence that I have not been useless to my generation. But, from circumstances, the main portion of my harvest is still on the ground, ripe indeed and only waiting, a few for the sickle, but a large part only for the *sheaving* and carting and housing—but from all this I must turn away and let them rot as they lie, and be as though they never had been ; for I must go and gather black berries and earth-nuts, or pick mushrooms and gild oak-apples for the palate and fancies of chance cus-tomers. I must abrogate the name of philosopher and poet, and scribble as fast as I can and with as little thought as I can for *Blackwood's Magazine,* or as I have been employed for the last days in writing MS. sermons for lazy clergymen who stipulate that the composition must be more than respectable.' . . . This " [*i.e.* to say this to myself] " I have not yet had courage to do. My soul sickens and my heart sinks, and thus oscillating between both " [forms of activity—the production of permanent and of ephemeral work] " I do neither—neither as it ought to be done to any profitable end."

And his proposal for extricating himself from this distressing position is that "those who think respect-fully and hope highly of my power and attainments should guarantee me a yearly sum for three or four years, adequate to my actual support, with such comforts and decencies of appearance as my health and habit have made necessaries, so that my mind may be un-

anxious as far as the present time is concerned." Thus
provided for he would undertake to devote two-thirds of
his time to some one work of those above mentioned—
that is to say, of the first four—and confine it exclusively
to it till finished, while the remaining third of his time
he would go on maturing and completing his "great
work," and "(for, if but easy in my mind, I have no
doubt either of the reawakening power or of the kindling
inclination) my *Christabel*, and what else the happier
hour may inspire." Mr. Green, he goes on to say, had
promised to contribute £30 to £40 yearly, another
pupil, "the son of one of my dearest old friends, £50,"
and £10 or £20 could, he thought, be relied on from
another. The whole amount of the required annuity
would be about £200, to be repaid of course should
disposal or sale of his works produce, or as far as they
should produce, the means. But "am I entitled," he
asks uneasily, "have I a *right* to do this? Can I do it
without moral degradation? And lastly, can it be done
without loss of character in the eyes of my acquaintances and of my friends' acquaintances?"

I cannot take upon myself to answer these painful
questions. The reply to be given to them must depend
upon the judgment which each individual student of this
remarkable but unhappy career may pass upon it as a
whole; and, while it would be too much to expect that
that judgment should be entirely favourable, one may
at least believe that a fair allowance for those inveterate
weaknesses of physical constitution which so largely
aggravated, if they did not wholly generate, the fatal
infirmities of Coleridge's moral nature, must materially
mitigate the harshness of its terms.

The story of Coleridge's closing years is soon told. It is mainly a record of days spent in meditation and discourse, in which character it will be treated of more fully in a subsequent chapter. His literary productions during the last fourteen years of his life were few in number, and but one of them of any great importance. In 1821 he had offered himself as an occasional contributor to *Blackwood's Magazine*, but a series of papers promised by him to that periodical were uncompleted, and his only two contributions (in October 1821 and January 1822) are of no particular note. In May 1825 he read a paper on the *Prometheus* of Æschylus before the Royal Society of Literature; but "the series of disquisitions respecting the Egyptian in connection with the sacerdotal theology and in contrast with the mysteries of ancient Greece," to which this essay had been announced as preparatory, never made their appearance. In the same year, however, he published one of the best known of his prose works, his *Aids to Reflection*.

Of the success of this latest of Coleridge's more important contributions to literature there can be no doubt. New editions of it seem to have been demanded at regular intervals for some twenty years after its first production, and it appears to have had during the same period a relatively equal reissue in the United States. The Rev. Dr. James Marsh, an American divine of some ability and reputation, composed a preliminary essay (now prefixed to the fifth English edition), in which he elaborately set forth the peculiar merits of the work, and undertook to initiate the reader in the fittest and most profitable method of making use of it. In these remarks the reverend essayist insists more strongly on the spirit-

ually edifying quality of the *Aids* than on their literary
merits, and, for my own part, I must certainly consider
him right in doing so.   As a religious manual it is easy
to understand how this volume of Coleridge's should
have obtained many and earnest readers.   What religious manual, which shows traces of spiritual insight, or
even merely of pious yearnings after higher and holier
than earthly things, has ever failed to win such readers
among the weary and heavy-laden of the world?   And
that Coleridge, a writer of the most penetrating glance
into divine mysteries, and writing always from a soul
all tremulous, as it were, with religious sensibility,
should have obtained such readers in abundance is not
surprising.   But to a critic and literary biographer I
cannot think that his success in this respect has much
to say.   For my own part, at any rate, I find considerable difficulty in tracing it to any distinctively literary
origin.   There seems to me to be less charm of thought,
less beauty of style, less even of Coleridge's seldom-fail-
ing force of effective statement, in the *Aids to Reflection*
than in almost any of his writings.   Even the volume of
some dozen short chapters on the Constitution of the
Church and State, published in 1830, as an " aid towards
a right judgment in the late Catholic Relief Bill," appears
to me to yield a more characteristic flavour of the
author's style, and to exhibit far more of his distinction
of literary workmanship than the earlier and more celebrated work.

Among the acquaintances made by Coleridge after
his retirement to Mr. Gillman's was one destined to be
of some importance to the history of his philosophical
work.   It was that of a gentleman whose name has

already been mentioned in this chapter, Mr. Joseph
Henry Green, afterwards a distinguished surgeon and
Fellow of the Royal Society, who in his early years had
developed a strong taste for metaphysical speculation,
going even so far as to devote one of his hard-earned
periods of professional holiday to a visit to Germany
for the sake of studying philosophy in that home of
abstract thought.   To him Coleridge was introduced by
his old Roman acquaintance, Ludwig Tieck, on one of
the latter's visits to England, and he became, as the
extract above quoted from Coleridge's correspondence
shows, his enthusiastic disciple and indefatigable fellow-
worker.   In the pursuit of their common studies and in
those weekly reunions of admiring friends which Coleridge, while his health permitted it, was in the habit of
holding, we may believe that a considerable portion of
these closing years of his life was passed under happier
conditions than he had been long accustomed to.   It is
pleasant to read of him among his birds and flowers,
and surrounded by the ever-watchful tendance of the
affectionate Gillmans, tranquil in mind at any rate, if not
at ease from his bodily ailments, and enjoying, as far
as enjoyment was possible to him, the peaceful close of
a stormy and unsettled day.   For the years 1825-30,
moreover, his pecuniary circumstances were improved
to the extent of £105 per annum, obtained for him at
the instance of the Royal Society of Literature, and
held by him till the death of George IV.

Two incidents of his later years are, however, worthy
of more special mention—a tour up the Rhine, which he
took in 1828, in company with Wordsworth and his
daughter ; and, some years earlier, a meeting with John

Keats. "A loose, slack, not well dressed youth," it is recorded in the *Table Talk*, published after his death by his nephew, "met Mr. ——" (it was Mr. Green, of whom more hereafter) "and myself in a lane near Highgate. Green knew him and spoke. It was Keats. He was introduced to me, and stayed a minute or so. After he had left us a little way, he came back and said, 'Let me carry away the memory, Coleridge, of having pressed your hand.' 'There is death in that hand,' I said to Green when Keats was gone; yet this was, I believe, before the consumption showed itself distinctly."

His own health, however, had been steadily declining in these latter years, and the German tour with the Wordsworths must, I should imagine, have been the last expedition involving any considerable exercise of the physical powers which he was able to take. Within a year or so afterwards his condition seems to have grown sensibly worse. In November 1831 he writes that for eighteen months past his life had been "one chain of severe sicknesses, brief and imperfect convalescences, and capricious relapses." Henceforth he was almost entirely confined to the sick-room. His faculties, however, still remained clear and unclouded. The entries in the *Table Talk* do not materially diminish in frequency. Their tone of colloquy undergoes no perceptible variation; they continue to be as stimulating and delightful reading as ever. Not till 11th July 1834 do we find any change; but here at last we meet the shadow, deemed longer than it was in reality, of the approaching end. "I am dying," said Coleridge, "but without expectation of a speedy release. Is it not strange that, very recently, bygone images and scenes of

early life have stolen into my mind like breezes blown
from the spice-islands of Youth and Hope—those twin
realities of the phantom world! I do not add Love,
for what is Love but Youth and Hope embracing, and,
so seen, as *one*. . . . Hooker wished to live to finish
his *Ecclesiastical Polity*—so I own I wish life and strength
had been spared to me to complete my *Philosophy*.
For, as God hears me, the originating, continuing,
and sustaining wish and design in my heart were to
exalt the glory of His name; and, which is the same
thing in other words, to promote the improvement of
mankind. But *visum aliter Deo*, and His will be done."

The end was nearer than he thought. It was on the
11th of July, as has been said, that he uttered these last
words of gentle and pious resignation. On that day
fortnight he died. Midway, however, in this intervening
period, he knew that the "speedy release" which he had
not ventured to expect was close at hand. The death,
when it came, was in some sort emblematic of the life.
Sufferings severe and constant, till within thirty-six
hours of the end : at the last peace. On the 25th of
July 1834 this sorely-tried, long-labouring, fate-marred
and self-marred life passed tranquilly away. The pitiful
words of Kent over his dead master rise irrepressibly to
the lips—

> " O let him pass : he hates him
> Who would upon the rack of this tough world
> Stretch him out longer."

There might have been something to be said, though not
by Kent, of the weaknesses of Lear himself ; but at such
a moment compassion both for the king and for the
poet may well impose silence upon censure.

CHAPTER XI.

Coleridge's metaphysics and theology—The *Spiritual Philosophy* of Mr. Green.

IN spite of all the struggles, the resolutions, and the entreaties which displayed themselves so distressingly in the letter to Mr. Allsop, quoted in the last chapter, it is doubtful whether Coleridge's "great work" made much additional progress during the last dozen years of his life. The weekly meeting with Mr. Green seems, according to the latter's biographer, to have been resumed. Mr. Simon tells us that he continued year after year to sit at the feet of his Gamaliel, getting more and more insight into his opinions, until, in 1834, two events occurred which determined the remaining course of Mr. Green's life. One of these events, it is needless to say, was Coleridge's death; the other was the death of his disciple's father, with the result of leaving Mr. Green possessed of such ample means as to render him independent of his profession. The language of Coleridge's will, together, no doubt, with verbal communications which had passed, imposed on Mr. Green what he accepted as an obligation to devote so far as necessary the whole remaining strength and earnestness of his life to the one task of systematising, developing, and establishing the doctrines of the Coleridgian philosophy. Accordingly, in 1836, two years after his master's death, he retired from medical practice, and thenceforward, until his own death nearly thirty years afterwards, he applied himself unceasingly to what was in a twofold sense a labour of love.

We are not, it seems from his biographer's account, to suppose that Mr. Green's task was in any material degree lightened for him by his previous collaboration with Coleridge. The latter had, as we have seen, declared in his letter to Allsop that "more than a volume" of the great work had been dictated by him to Mr. Green, so as to exist in a condition fit for the press : but this, according to Mr. Simon, was not the case ; and the probability is therefore that "more than a volume" meant written material equal in amount to more than a volume—of course, an entirely different thing. Mr. Simon, at any rate, assures us that no available written material existed for setting comprehensively before the public, in Coleridge's own language, and in an argued form, the philosophical system with which he wished his name to be identified. Instead of it there were fragments —for the most part mutually inadaptable fragments, and beginnings, and studies of special subjects, and number-less notes on the margins and fly-leaves of books.

With this equipment, such as it was, Mr. Green set to work to methodise the Coleridgian doctrines, and to construct from them nothing less than such a system of philosophy as should "virtually include the law and explanation of all being, conscious and unconscious, and of all correlativity and duty, and be applicable directly

or by deduction to whatsoever the human mind can
contemplate—sensuous or supersensuous—of experience,
purpose, or imagination." Born under post - diluvian
conditions, Mr. Green was of course unable to accomplish his self-proposed enterprise, but he must be allowed to have attacked his task with remarkable energy.
"Theology, ethics, politics and political history, eth-
nology, language, æsthetics, psychology, physics, and the
allied sciences, biology, logic, mathematics, pathology,
all these subjects," declares his biographer, "were
thoughtfully studied by him, in at least their basial
principles and metaphysics, and most were elaborately
written of, as though for the divisions of some vast
cyclopædic work." At an early period of his labours he
thought it convenient to increase his knowledge of
Greek; he began to study Hebrew when more than
sixty years old, and still later in life he took up Sanscrit.
It was not until he was approaching his seventieth year
and found his health beginning to fail him that Mr.
Green seems to have felt that his design, in its more
ambitious scope, must be abandoned, and that, in the
impossibility of applying the Coleridgian system of
philosophy to all human knowledge, it was his imperative duty under his literary trust to work out that
particular application of it which its author had most at
heart. Already, in an unpublished work which he had
made it the first care of his trusteeship to compose, he
had, though but roughly and imperfectly, as he considered, exhibited the relation of his master's doctrines
to revealed religion, and it had now become time to
supersede this unpublished compendium, the *Religio
Laici*, as he had styled it, by a fuller elaboration of the

great Coleridgian position, that "Christianity, rightly understood, is identical with the highest philosophy, and that, apart from all question of historical evidence, the essential doctrines of Christianity are necessary and eternal truths of reason — truths which man, by the vouchsafed light of Nature and without aid from documents or tradition, may always and anywhere discover for himself." To this work accordingly Mr. Green devoted the few remaining years of his life, and, dying in 1863 at the age of seventy-two, left behind him in MS. the work entitled *Spiritual Philosophy : founded on the teaching of the late Samuel Taylor Coleridge,* which was published two years later, together with the memoir of the author, from which I have quoted, by Mr. John Simon. It consists of two volumes, the first of which is devoted to the exposition of the general principles of Coleridge's philosophy, while the second is entirely theological, and aims at indicating on principles for which the first volume has contended, the essential doctrines of Christianity.

The earlier chapters of this volume Mr. Green devotes to an exposition (if indeed the word can be applied to what is really a catalogue of the results of a transcendental intuition) of the essential difference between the reason and the understanding—a distinction which Coleridge has himself elsewhere described as preeminently the *gradus ad philosophiam,* and might well have called its *pons asinorum.* In the second part of his first volume Mr. Green applies himself to the establishment of a position which, fundamental as it must be accounted in all philosophical speculations of this school, is absolutely vital to the theology which Coleridge sought to erect upon a metaphysical basis. This position is that the human will is to be regarded as the one ultimate fact of self-consciousness. So long as man confines himself to the contemplation of his percipient and reflective self alone—so long as he attends only to those modes of consciousness which are produced in him by the impressions of the senses and the operations of thought, he can never hope to escape from the famous *reductio ad inscibile* of Hume. He can never affirm anything more than the existence of those modes of consciousness, or assert, at least as a direct deliverance of intuition, that his conscious self *is* anything apart from the perceptions and concepts to which he is attending. But when he turns from his perceiving and thinking to his willing self he becomes for the first time aware of something deeper than the mere objective presentations of consciousness; he obtains a direct intuition of an originant, causative, and independent self-existence. He will have attained in short to the knowledge of a noumenon, and of the only knowable noumenon. The barrier, elsewhere insuperable between the subject and object, is broken down; that which *knows* becomes identified with that which *is;* and in the consciousness of will the consciousness also of a self, as something independent of and superior to its own modifications, is not so much affirmed as acquired. The essence, in short, of the Coleridgian ontology consists in the alteration of a single though a very important word in the well known Cartesian formula. *Cogito ergo sum* had been shown by Hume to involve an illicit process of reasoning. Descartes, according to the Scottish sceptic, had no right to have said more than *Cogito ergo cogitationes sunt.* But substitute willing for thinking, convert the formula into *Volo ergo sum*, and it becomes irrefragable.

So far as I can perceive, it would have been sufficient for Mr. Green's subsequent argument to have thus established the position of the will as the ultimate fact of consciousness, but he goes on to assert that he has thus secured the immovable ground of a philosophy of Realism. For since man, "in affirming his Personality by the verb substantive I am, asserts, nay, acquires, the knowledge of his own Substance as a Spiritual being, and thereby knows what substance truly and properly is—so he contemplates the outward, persons or things, as subjects partaking of reality by virtue of the same substance of which he is conscious in his own person." So far, however, from this being a philosophy of Realism, it is in effect, if not indeed in actual terms, a philosophy of Idealism. I, at least, am unable to see how any Idealist, from Berkeley downwards, could ask for a better definition of his theory of the external world than that it "partakes of reality by virtue of the same substance of which he is conscious in his own person."

But it is, of course, with the second volume of Mr. Green's work that one is chiefly concerned. Had Coleridge been a mere Transcendentalist for Transcendentalism's sake, had there been no connection between his philosophy of Being and his religious creed, it might be a question whether even the highly condensed and necessarily imperfect sketch which has here been given of it would not have been superfluous and out of place. But Coleridge was a Theosophist first, and a philosopher afterwards; it was mainly as an organon of religion that he valued his philosophy, and it was to the development and perfection of it, *as such organon*, that he may be said to have devoted, so far as it could be redeemed from its enthralment to lower necessities, the whole of the latter half of his career.   No account of his life, therefore, could be complete without at least some brief glance at the details of this notable attempt to lead the world to true religion by the road of the Transcendental philosophy.   It is difficult, of course, for those who have been trained in a wholly different school of thought to do justice to processes of reasoning carried on, as they cannot but hold, in terms of the inconceivable ; it is still more difficult to be *sure* that you have done justice to it after all has been said ; and I think that no candid student of the Coleridgian philosophico-theology (not being a professed disciple of it, and therefore bound, at any rate, to feign familiarity with incomprehensibilities) will deny that he is often compelled to formulate its positions and recite its processes in somewhat of the same modest and confiding spirit as animates those youthful geometricians who learn their Euclid by heart. With this proviso I will, as briefly as may be, trace the course of the dialectic by which Mr. Green seeks to make the Coleridgian metaphysics demonstrative of the truth of Christianity.

Having shown that the Will is the true and the only tenable base of Philosophic Realism, the writer next proceeds to explain the growth of the Soul, from its rudimental strivings in its fallen condition to the development of its spiritual capabilities, and to trace its ascent to the conception of the Idea of God.   The argument—if we may apply so definite a name to a process which is continually forced to appeal to something that may perhaps be higher, but is certainly *other* than the ratiocinative faculty—is founded partly on moral and partly on intellectual considerations. By an analysis of the moral phenomena associated with the action of the human will, and, in particular, of the conflict which arises between "the tendency of all Will to make itself absolute," and the consciousness that, under the conditions of man's fallen state, nothing but misery could result both to the individual and the race from the fulfilment of this tendency,—Mr. Green shows how the Soul, or the Reason, or the Speculative Intellect (for he seems to use all three expressions indiscriminately) is morally prepared for the reception of the truth which his Understanding alone could never have compassed,—the Idea of God. This is in effect neither more nor less than a restatement of that time-honoured argument for the existence of some Being of perfect holiness which has always weighed so much with men of high spirituality as to blind them to the fact of its actually enhancing the intellectual difficulties of the situation. Man possesses a Will which longs to fulfil itself ; but it is coupled with a nature which constantly impels him to those gratifications of will which tend not to self-preservation and progress, but to their contraries. Surely, then, on the strength of the mere law of life, which prevails everywhere, there must be some higher archetypal Will, to which human wills, or rather certain selected examples of them, may more and more conform themselves, and in which the union of unlimited efficiency in operation with unqualified purity of aim has been once for all effected. Or to put it yet another way : The life of the virtuous man is a life auxiliary to the preservation

and progress of the race ; but his will is under restraint.
The will of the vicious man energises freely enough,
but his life is hostile to the preservation and progress of
the race.   Now the natural and essential *nisus* of all
Will is towards absolute freedom.   But nothing in life
has a natural and essential *nisus* towards that which
tends to its deterioration and extinction.   Therefore,
there must be some ultimate means of reconciling absolute freedom of the Will with perfectly salutary conditions of its exercise.   And since Mr. Green, like his
master and all other Platonists, is incapable of stopping
here, and contenting himself with assuming the existence
of a "stream of tendency" which will gradually bring
the human will into the required conditions, he here
makes the inevitable Platonic jump, and proceeds to
conclude that there must be a self-existent ideal Will in
which absolute freedom and power concur with perfect
purity and holiness.

So much for the moral part of Mr. Green's proof,
which so far fails, it will be observed, to carry us much
beyond the Pantheistic position.   It has, that is to say,
to be proved that the "power not ourselves," which has
been called Will, originates in some source to which we
should be rationally justified in giving the name of
"God ; " and, singular as such a thing may seem, it is
impossible at any rate for the logic of the understanding
to regard Mr. Green's argument on this point as otherwise than hopelessly circular.   The half-dozen pages or
so which he devotes to the refutation of the Pantheistic
view reduce themselves to the following simple *petitio
principii :* the power is first assumed to be a Will ; it is
next affirmed with perfect truth that the very notion

of Will would escape us except under the condition of Personality; and from this the existence of a personal God as the source of the power in question deduced. And the same vice underlies the further argument by which Mr. Green meets the familiar objection to the personality of the Absolute as involving contradictory conceptions. An infinite Person, he argues, is no contradiction in terms, unless "finition or limitation" be regarded as identical with "negation" (which, when applied to a hypothetical Infinite, one would surely think it is); and an Absolute Will is not the less absolute from being self-determined *ab intrâ*. For how, he asks, can any Will which is causative of reality be conceived as a Will except by conceiving it as *se finiens*, predetermining itself to the specific processes required by the act of causation? How, indeed? But the answer of a Pantheist would of course be that the very impossibility of conceiving of Will except as *se finiens* is his very ground for rejecting the notion of a volitional (in the sense of a personal) origin of the cosmos.

However, it is beyond my purposes to enter into any detailed criticism of Mr. Green's position, more especially as I have not yet reached the central and capital point of his spiritual philosophy—the construction of the Christian theology on the basis of the Coleridgian metaphysics. Having deduced the Idea of God from man's consciousness of an individual Will perpetually affirming itself, Mr. Green proceeds to evolve the Idea of the Trinity, by (as he considers it) an equally necessary process from two of the invariable accompaniments of the above-mentioned introspective act. "For as in our consciousness," he truly says, "we are under the necessity of distinguishing the relation of "myself," now as the *subject* thinking and now as the *object* contemplated in the manifold of thought, so we might express the relations in the Divine instance as *Deus Subjectivus* and *Deus Objectivus*,—that is, the Absolute Subjectivity or Supreme Will, uttering itself as and contemplating itself in the Absolute Objectivity or plenitude of Being eternally and causatively realised in his Personality." Whence it follows (so runs or seems to run the argument) that the Idea of God the Father as necessarily involves the Idea of God the Son as the "I" who, as the thinking subject, contemplate myself, implies the contemplated "Me" as the object thought of. Again, the man who reflects on the fact of his consciousness, "which discloses to him the unavoidable opposition of subject and object in the self of which he is conscious, cannot fail to see that the conscious mind requires not only the distinction in order to the act of reflection in itself, but the continual sense of the relative nature of the distinction and of the essential oneness of the mind itself." Whence it follows (so runs or seems to run the argument) that the Idea of the first two Persons of the Trinity as necessarily involves the Idea of the Third Person, as the contemplation of the "Me" by the "I" implies the perpetual consciousness that the contemplator and the contemplated—the "I" and the "Me"—are one. In this manner is the Idea of the Trinity shown to be involved in the Idea of God, and to arise out of it by an implication as necessary as that which connects together the three phases of consciousness attendant upon every self-contemplative act of the individual mind.[1]

---

[1] Were it not hazardous to treat processes of the Speculative Reason as we deal with the vulgar dialectic of the Understanding,

It may readily be imagined that after the Speculative
Reason has been made to perform such feats as these the
remainder of the work proposed to it could present no
serious difficulty.   And in the half-dozen chapters which
follow it is made to evolve in succession the doctrine of
the Incarnation, the Advent, and the Atonement of
Christ, and to explain the mysteries of the fall of man
and of original sin.   Considered in the aspect in which
Coleridge himself would have preferred to regard his
pupil's work, namely as a systematic attempt to lead the
minds of men to Christianity by an intellectual route,
no more hopeless enterprise perhaps could have been
conceived than that embodied in these volumes.   It is
like offering a traveller a guide-book written in hiero-
glyphics.   Upon the most liberal computation it is probable that not one-fourth part of educated mankind are
capable of so much as comprehending the philosophic
doctrine upon which Coleridge seeks to base Christianity,
and it is doubtful whether any but a still smaller
fraction of these would admit that the foundation was
capable of supporting the superstructure.   That the
writings of the pupil, like the teachings of the master
whom he interprets, may serve the cause of religion
in another than an intellectual way is possible enough.
Not a few of the functions assigned to the Speculative

one would be disposed to reply that if the above argument proves
the existence of three persons in the Godhead, it must equally prove
the existence of three persons in every man who reflects upon his
conscious self.   That the Divine Mind, when engaged in the act of
self-contemplation, must be conceived under three *relations* is doubtless as true as that the human mind, when so engaged, must be so
conceived ; but that these three *relations* are so many objective
realities is what Mr. Green asserts indeed a few pages farther on,
but what he nowhere attempts to prove.

Reason will strike many of us as moral and spiritual rather than intellectual in their character, and the appeal to them is in fact an appeal to man to chasten the lower passions of his nature, and to discipline his unruly will. Exhortations of that kind are religious all the world of philosophy over, and will succeed in proportion to the moral fervour and oratorical power which distinguish them. But if the benefits of Coleridge's theological teachings are to be reduced to this, it would of course have been much better to have dissociated them altogether from the exceedingly abstruse metaphysic to which they have been wedded.

CHAPTER XII.

Coleridge's position in his later years—His discourse—His influence on contemporary thought—Final review of his intellectual work.

THE critic who would endeavour to appreciate the position which Coleridge fills in the history of literature and thought for the first half of the nineteenth century must, if he possesses ordinary candour and courage, begin, I think, with a confession. He must confess an inability to comprehend the precise manner in which that position was attained, and the precise grounds on which it was recognised. For vast as were Coleridge's powers of thought and expression, and splendid, if incomplete, as is the record which they have left behind them in his works, they were never directed to purposes of instruction or persuasion in anything like that systematic and concentrated manner which is necessary to him who would found a school. Coleridge's writings on philosophical and theological subjects were essentially discursive, fragmentary, incomplete. Even when he professes an intention of exhausting his subject and affects a logical arrangement, it is not long before he forgets the design and departs from the order. His disquisitions are in no sense connected treatises on the subjects to which they relate. Brilliant *aperçus*, gnomic sayings, flights of fervid eloquence, infinitely suggestive reflections—of these there is enough and to spare; but these, though an ample equipment for the critic, are not sufficient for the constructive philosopher. Nothing, it must be frankly said, in Coleridge's philosophical and theological writings—nothing, that is to say, which appeals in them to the mere intelligence—suffices to explain, at least to the appreciation of posterity, the fact that he was surrounded during these closing years of his life by an eager crowd of real or supposed disciples, including two, at any rate, of the most remarkable personalities of the time. And if nothing in Coleridge's writings serves to account for it, so neither does anything traceable or tangible in the mere matter of his conversations. This last point, however, is one which must be for the present reserved. I wish for the moment to confine myself to the fact of Coleridge's position during his later life at Highgate. To this we have, as we all know, an extremely eminent witness, and one from whose evidence most people, one may suppose, are by this time able to make their own deductions in all matters relating to the persons with whom he was brought into contact. Carlyle on Charles Lamb, few as the sour sentences are, must always warn us to be careful how we follow Carlyle " on" anybody whomsoever. But there is no evidence of any ill feeling on Carlyle's part towards Coleridge — nothing but a humorous, kindly-contemptuous compassion for his weaknesses and eccentricities; and the famous description in the *Life of Sterling* may be taken therefore as a fairly accurate account of the man and the circumstances to which it refers :—

"Coleridge sat on the brow of Highgate Hill in those years, looking down on London and its smoke tumult like a sage escaped from the inanity of life's battle, attracting towards him the thoughts of innumerable brave souls still engaged there. His express contributions to poetry, philosophy, or any specific province of human literature or enlightenment had been small and sadly intermittent; but he had, especially among young inquiring men, a higher than literary, a kind of prophetic or magician character. He was thought to hold— he alone in England—the key of German and other Transcendentalisms; knew the sublime secret of believing by the 'reason' what the 'understanding' had been obliged to fling out as incredible; and could still, after Hume and Voltaire had done their best and worst with him, profess himself an orthodox Christian, and say and print to the Church of England, with its singular old rubrics and surplices at Allhallowtide, *Esto perpetua*. A sublime man; who alone in those dark days had saved his crown of spiritual manhood, escaping from the black materialisms and revolutionary deluges with 'God, Freedom, Immortality,' still his; a king of men. The practical intellects of the world did not much heed him, or carelessly reckoned him a metaphysical dreamer; but to the rising spirits of the young generation he had this dusky sublime character, and sat there as a kind of Magus, girt in mystery and enigma; his Dodona oak-grove (Mr. Gillman's house at Highgate) whispering strange things, uncertain whether oracles or jargon."

The above quotation would suffice for my immediate purpose, but it is impossible to deny oneself or one's readers the pleasure of a refreshed recollection of the noble landscape - scene and the masterly portrait that follow :

" The Gillmans did not encourage much company or excitation of any sort round their sage ; nevertheless, access to him, if a youth did reverently wish it, was not difficult. He would stroll about the pleasant garden with you, sit in the pleasant rooms of the place—perhaps take you to his own peculiar room, high up, with a rearward view, which was the chief view of all. A really charming outlook in fine weather. Close at hand wide sweeps of flowing leafy gardens, their few houses mostly hidden, the very chimney-pots veiled under blossoming umbrage, flowed gloriously down hill ; gloriously issuing in wide-tufted undulating plain country, rich in all charms of field and town. Waving blooming country of the brightest green, dotted all over with hand-some villas, handsome groves crossed by roads and human traffic, here inaudible, or heard only as a musical hum ; and behind all swam, under olive-tinted haze, the illimitable limitary ocean of London, with its domes and steeples definite in the sun, big Paul's and the many memories attached to it hanging high over all. Nowhere of its kind could you see a grander prospect on a bright summer day, with the set of the air going southward—southward, and so draping with the city smoke not *you* but the city."

Then comes the invariable final touch, the one dash of black—or green, shall we call it—without which the master left no picture that had a human figure in the foreground :—

" Here for hours would Coleridge talk concerning all conceivable or inconceivable things ; and liked nothing better than to have an intelligent, or, failing that, even a silent and patient human listener. He distinguished himself to all that ever heard him as at least the most surprising talker extant in this world,—and to some small minority, by no means to all, as the most excellent."

Then follows the well-known, wonderfully vivid, cynically pathetic, sketch of the man :—

" The good man—he was now getting old, towards sixty perhaps, and gave you the idea of a life that had been full of sufferings ; a life heavy-laden, half-vanquished, still swim-ming painfully in seas of manifold physical and other be-

wilderment. Brow and head were round and of massive
weight, but the face was flabby and irresolute. The deep
eyes, of a light hazel, were as full of sorrow as of inspiration ;
confused pain looked mildly from them, as in a kind of mild
astonishment. The whole figure and air, good and amiable
otherwise, might be called flabby and irresolute ; expressive
of weakness under possibility of strength. He hung loosely
on his limbs, with knees bent, and stooping attitude ; in
walking he rather shuffled than decisively stept ; and a lady
once remarked he never could fix which side of the garden-
walk would suit him best, but continually shifted, corkscrew
fashion, and kept trying both ; a heavy-laden, high-aspiring,
and surely much-suffering man. His voice, naturally soft and
good, had contracted itself into a plaintive snuffle and sing-
song ; he spoke as if preaching—you could have said preaching
earnestly and almost .hopelessly the weightiest things.   I
still recollect his ‘ object ’ and ‘ subject,’ terms of continual
recurrence in the Kantean province ; and how he sang and
snuffled them into ‘ om-m-ject’ and ‘ sum-m-mject,’ with
a kind of solemn shake or quaver as he rolled along.[1]   No
talk in his century or in any other could be more surprising.”

Such, as he appeared to this half-contemptuous, half-
compassionate, but ever acute observer, was Coleridge
at this the zenith of his influence over the nascent
thought of his day.   Such to Carlyle seemed the *manner* of
the deliverance of the oracles ; in his view of their matter,
as we all know from an equally well-remembered passage, his tolerance disappears, and his account here, with

[1] No one who recollects the equally singular manner in which
another most distinguished metaphysician—the late Dean Mansel
—was wont to quaver forth his admirably turned and often highly
eloquent phrases of philosophical exposition, can fail to be reminded
of him by the above description. No two temperaments or his-
tories however could be more dissimilar. The two philosophers
resembled each other in nothing save the “ om-mject ” and
sum-mject ” of their studies.

all its racy humour, is almost wholly impatient. Talk,
"suffering no interruption, however reverent," "hastily
putting aside all foreign additions, annotation, or most
ingenuous desires for elucidation, as well-meant super-
fluities which would never do ;" talk "not flowing any-
whither, like a river, but spreading everywhither in in-
extricable currents and regurgitations like a lake or
sea ;" a "confused unintelligible flood of utterance,
threatening to submerge all known landmarks of thought
and drown the world with you"—this, it must be admitted, is not an easily recognisable description of the
Word of Life.   Nor, certainly, does Carlyle's own personal experience of its preaching and effects—he having
heard the preacher talk "with eager musical energy
two stricken hours, his face radiant and moist, and com-
municate no meaning whatsoever to any individual of his
hearers,"—certain of whom, the narrator for one, "still
kept eagerly listening in hope, while the most had long
before given up and formed (if the room was large
enough) humming groups of their own."   "He began
anywhere," continues this irresistibly comic sketch ; "you
put some question to him, made some suggestive observation ; instead of answering this, or decidedly setting
out towards an answer of it, he would accumulate formidable apparatus, logical swim-bladders, transcendental life-
preservers, and other precautionary and vehiculatory
gear for setting out ; perhaps did at last get under way
—but was swiftly solicited, turned aside by the flame of
some radiant new game on this hand or on that into new
courses, and ever into new ; and before long into all the
universe, where it was uncertain what game you would
catch, or whether any."   He had, indeed, according to the

dissatisfied listener, "not the least talent for explaining
this or anything to them ; and you swam and fluttered
on the mistiest, wide, unintelligible deluge of things for
most part in a rather profitless uncomfortable manner."
And the few vivid phrases of eulogy which follow seem
only to deepen by contrast the prevailing hue of the
picture. The "glorious islets" which were sometimes
seen to "rise out of the haze," the "balmy sunny islets
of the blest and the intelligible, at whose emergence
the secondary humming group would all cease humming
and hang breathless upon the eloquent words, till once
your islet got wrapped in the mist again, and they would
recommence humming"—these, it seems to be suggested,
but rarely revealed themselves; but "eloquent, artisti-
cally expressive words you always had; piercing radiances
of a most subtle insight came at intervals ; tones of noble
pious sympathy recognisable as pious though strangely
coloured, were never wanting long; but, in general, you
could not call this aimless cloud-capt, cloud-bound, law-
lessly meandering discourse, by the name of excellent
talk, but only of surprising. . . .   The moaning sing-
song of that theosophico-metaphysical monotony left in
you at last a very dreary feeling."

It is tolerably clear, I think, that some considerable
discount must be allowed upon the sum of disparage-
ment in this famous criticism.   We have learnt, indeed,
to be more on the look-out for the disturbing influences
of temperament in the judgments of this atrabilious observer than was the case when the *Life of Sterling* was
written, and it is difficult to doubt that the unfavourable strokes in the above-quoted description have been
unduly multiplied and deepened, partly in the mere

waywardness of a sarcastic humour, and partly perhaps from a less excusable cause.   It is always dangerous to accept one remarkable talker's view of the characteristics of another ; and if this is true of men who merely compete with each other in the ordinary give-and-take of the dinner-table epigrammatist and *raconteur*, the caution is doubly necessary in the case of two rival prophets—two competing oracles.   There are those among us who hold that the conversation of the Chelsea sage, in his later years, resembled his own description of the Highgate philosopher's, in this, at any rate, that it was mightily intolerant of interruption ; and one is apt to suspect that at no time of his life did Carlyle "understand duologue" much better than Coleridge.   It is probable enough, therefore, that the young lay-preacher did not quite relish being silenced by the elder, and that his account of the sermons was coloured by the recollection that his own remained undelivered.   There is an abundance of evidence that the "glorious islets" emerged far more often from the transcendental haze than Carlyle would have us suppose.   Hazlitt, a bitter assailant of Coleridge's, and whose caustic remark that "his talk was excellent if you let him start from no premisses and come to no conclusion" is cited with approval by Carlyle, has elsewhere spoken of Coleridge as the only person from whom he ever learned anything, has said of him that though he talked on for ever you wished him to talk on for ever, that "his thoughts did not seem to come with labour and effort, but as if borne on the gusts of genius, and as if the wings of his imagination lifted him from his feet."   And besides this testimony to the eloquence which Carlyle

only but inadequately recognises, one should set for
what it is worth De Quincey's evidence to that consequence of thought which Carlyle denies altogether.   To
De Quincey the complaint that Coleridge wandered in
his talk appeared unjust.   According to him the great
discourser only "seemed to wander," and he seemed to
wander the most "when in fact his resistance to the
wandering instinct was greatest, viz. when the compass
and huge circuit by which his illustrations moved travelled farthest into remote regions before they began to
revolve.   Long before this coming round commenced
most people had lost him, and, naturally enough, supposed that he had lost himself.   They continued to
admire the separate beauty of the thoughts, but did not
see their relations to the dominant theme."   De Quincey
however, declares positively in the faith of his "long
and intimate knowledge of Coleridge's mind, that logic
the most severe was as inalienable from his modes of
thinking as grammar from his language."

Nor should we omit the testimony of another, a more
partial, perhaps, but even better informed judge.   The
Table Talk, edited by Mr. Nelson Coleridge, shows how
pregnant, how pithy, how full of subtle observation, and
often also of playful humour, could be the talk of
the great discourser in its lighter and more colloquial
forms.   The book indeed is, to the thinking of one, at
any rate, of its frequent readers, among the most delightful in the world.   But thus speaks its editor of his uncle's
conversation in his more serious moods :—

   " To pass an entire day with Coleridge was a marvellous
change indeed [from the talk of daily life].   It was a
Sabbath past expression, deep and tranquil and serene.

You came to a man who had travelled in many countries and
in critical times ; who had seen and felt the world in most
of its ranks and in many of its vicissitudes and weaknesses ;
one to whom all literature and art were absolutely subject ;
and to whom, with a reasonable allowance as to technical
details, all science was, in a most extraordinary degree,
familiar.   Throughout a long-drawn summer's day would this
man talk to you in low, equable, but clear and musical tones
concerning things human and divine ; marshalling all history, harmonising all experiment, probing the depths of your
consciousness, and revealing visions of glory and terror to
the imagination ; but pouring withal such floods of light
upon the mind that you might for a season, like Paul, become
blind in the very act of conversion.   And this he would do
without so much as one allusion to himself, without a word of
reflection upon others, save when any given art fell naturally
in the way of his discourse ; without one anecdote that was
not proof and illustration of a previous position ;—gratifying
no passion, indulging no caprice, but, with a calm mastery
over your soul, leading you onward and onward for ever
through a thousand windings, yet with no pause, to some
magnificent point in which, as in a focus, all the parti-
coloured rays of his discourse should converge in light.   In
all these he was, in truth, your teacher and guide ; but in
a little while you might forget that he was other than a
fellow-student and the companion of your way—so playful
was his manner, so simple his language, so affectionate the
glance of his eye ! "

Impressive, however, as these displays may have
been, it is impossible to suppose that their direct didactic value as discourses was at all considerable.   Such
as it was, moreover, it was confined in all probability to
an extremely select circle of followers.   A few mystics
of the type of Maurice, a few eager seekers after truth
like Sterling, may have gathered, or fancied they
gathered, distinct dogmatic instruction from the Highgate oracles ; and no doubt, to the extent of his influ-

ence over the former of these disciples, we may justly
credit Coleridge's discourses with having exercised a real
if only a transitory directive effect upon nineteenth-cen-
tury thought.   But the terms in which his influence is
sometimes spoken of appear, as far as one can judge of
the matter at this distance of time, to be greatly exaggerated.   To speak of it in the same way as we are—
or were—accustomed to speak of the influence of Carlyle,
is to subject it to an altogether inappropriate comparison.
It is not merely that Coleridge founded no recognisable
school, for neither did Carlyle.   It is that the former
can show absolutely nothing at all resembling that sort
of power which enabled the latter to lay hold upon all
the youthful minds of his time—minds of the most
disparate orders and associated with the utmost diversi-
ties of temperament, and detain them in a captivity
which, brief as it may have been in some cases, has in
no case failed to leave its marks behind it.   Over a few
spirits already prepared to receive them Coleridge's
teachings no doubt exerted power, but he led no soul
captive against its will.   There are few middle-aged
men of active intelligence at the present day who can
avoid a confession of having " taken " Carlylism in their
youth; but no mental constitutions not predisposed to it
could ever have caught Coleridgism at all.   There is
indeed no moral theory of life, there are no maxims
of conduct, such as youth above all things craves for, in
Coleridge's teaching.   Apart from the intrinsic difficulties
of the task to which he invites his disciples, it labours
under a primary and essential disadvantage of postpon-
ing moral to intellectual liberation.   Contrive somehow
or other to attain to just ideas as to the capacities and

limitations of the human consciousness, considered especially in relation to its two important and eternally
distinct functions, the Reason and the Understanding:
and peace of mind shall in due time be added unto
you. That is in effect Coleridge's answer to the inquirer
who consults him; and if the distinction between the
Reason and the Understanding were as obvious as it is
obscure to the average unmetaphysical mind, and of a
value as assured for the purpose to which Coleridge
applies it as it is uncertain, the answer would nevertheless send many a would-be disciple sorrowful away.
His natural impulse is to urge the oracle to tell him
whether there be not some one moral attitude which he
can wisely and worthily adopt towards the universe,
whatever theory he may form of his mental relations to
it, or without forming any such theory at all. And it
was because Carlyle supplied, or was believed to supply
an answer, such as it was, to this universal question, that
his train of followers, voluntary and involuntary, permanent and temporary, has been so large.

It appears to me, therefore, on as careful an examination of the point as the data admit of, that Coleridge's
position in these latter days of his life has been somewhat mythically exalted by the generation which succeeded him. There are, I think, distinct traces of a
Coleridgian legend which has only slowly died out.
The actual truth I believe to be that Coleridge's position from 1818 or 1820 till his death, though one of
the greatest eminence, was in no sense one of the highest,
or even of any considerable influence. Fame and honour,
in the fullest measure, were no doubt his : in that matter,
indeed, he was only receiving payment of long-delayed

arrears. The poetic school with which he was, though
not with entire accuracy, associated had outlived its
period of contempt and obloquy. In spite of the two
quarterlies, the Tory review hostile, its Whig rival coldly
silent, the public had recognised the high imaginative
merit of *Christabel ;* and who knows but that if the first
edition of the *Lyrical Ballads* had appeared at this date
instead of twenty years before, it would have obtained
a certain number of readers even among landsmen ?[1]
But over and above the published works of the poet
there were those extraordinary personal characteristics
to which the fame of his works of course attracted a far
larger share than formerly of popular attention. A
remarkable man has more attractive power over the
mass of mankind than the most remarkable of books,
and it was because the report of Coleridge among those
who knew him was more stimulating to public curiosity
than even the greatest of his poems, that his celebrity
in these latter years attained such proportions. Wordsworth said that though "he had seen many men do
wonderful things, Coleridge was the only wonderful
man he had ever met," and it was not the doer of
wonderful things but the wonderful man that English
society in those days went out for to see. Seeing would
have been enough, but for a certain number there was
hearing too, with the report of it for all ; and it is not
surprising that fame of the marvellous discourser should,
in mere virtue of his extraordinary power of improvised
speech, his limitless and untiring mastery of articulate

---

[1] The Longmans told Coleridge that the greater part of the
first edition of the *Lyrical Ballads* had been sold to seafaring men,
who, having heard of the *Ancient Mariner*, took the volume for a
naval song-book.

words, have risen to a height to which writers whose only voice is in their pens can never hope to attain.

A reputation of that kind, however, must necessarily perish with its possessor; and Coleridge's posthumous renown has grown, his place in English literature has become more assured, if it has not been even fixed higher, since his death than during his lifetime. This is, in part no doubt, one among the consequences of those very defects of character which so unfortunately limited his actual achievements. He has been credited by faith, as it were, with those famous "unwritten books" of which he assured Charles Lamb that the titles alone would fill a volume, and such "popular reputation," in the strict sense of the word, as he has left behind him, is measured rather by what he was thought capable of doing than by what he did. By serious students, however, the real worth of Coleridge will be differently estimated. For them his peculiar value to English literature is not only undiminished by the incompleteness of his work; it has been, in a certain sense, enhanced thereby. Or, perhaps, it would be more strictly accurate to say that the value could not have existed without the incompleteness. A Coleridge with the faculty of concentration, and the habit of method superadded—a Coleridge capable of becoming possessed by any one form of intellectual energy to the exclusion of all others—might, indeed, have left behind him a more enduring reputation as a philosopher, and possibly (although this, for reasons already stated, is, in my own opinion, extremely doubtful bequeathed to his countrymen more poetry destined to live; but, unquestionably, he would never have been able to render that precise service to

modern thought and literature which, in fact, they owe
to him.   To have exercised his vivifying and fertilising
influence over the minds of others his intellect was
bound to be of the dispersive order ; it was essential
that he should " take all knowledge to be his province,"
and that that eager, subtle, and penetrative mind should
range as freely as it did over subject after subject of human
interest ;—illuminating each of them in turn with those
rays of true critical insight which, amid many bewildering cross-lights and some few downright *ignes fatui*,
flash forth upon us from all Coleridge's work.

Of the personal weaknesses which prevented the just
development of the powers, enough, perhaps, has been
incidentally said in the course of this volume.   But, in
summing up his history, I shall not, I trust, be thought
to judge the man too harshly in saying that, though the
natural disadvantages of wretched health, almost from
boyhood upward, must, in common fairness, be admitted
in partial excuse for his failure, they do not excuse it altogether.   It is difficult not to feel that Coleridge's character,
apart altogether from defects of physical constitution,
was wanting in manliness of fibre.   His willingness to
accept assistance at the hands of others is too manifestly
displayed even at the earlier and more robust period of
his life.   It would be a mistake, of course, in dealing
with a literary man of Coleridge's era, to apply the same
standards as obtain in our own days.   Wordsworth, as we
have seen, made no scruple to accept the benevolences
of the Wedgwoods.   Southey, the type of independence and self-help, was, for some years, in receipt of a
pension from a private source.   But Coleridge, as Miss
Meteyard's disclosures have shown, was at all times far

more willing to depend upon others, and was far less scrupulous about soliciting their bounty, than was either of his two friends. Had he shared more of the spirit which made Johnson refuse to owe to the benevolence of others what Providence had enabled him to do for himself, it might have been better, no doubt, for the world and for the work which he did therein.

But when we consider what that work was, how varied and how wonderful, it seems idle—nay, it seems ungrateful and ungracious — to speculate too curiously on what further or other benefits this great intellect might have conferred upon mankind, had its possessor been endowed with those qualities of resolution and independence which he lacked. That Coleridge so often only *shows* the way, and so seldom guides our steps along it to the end, is no just ground of complaint. It would be as unreasonable to complain of a beacon-light that it is not a steam-tug, and forget in the incompleteness of its separate services the glory of their number. It is a more reasonable objection that the light itself is too often liable to obscuration,—that it stands erected upon a rock too often enshrouded by the mists of its encircling sea. But even this objection should not too greatly weigh with us. It would be wiser and better for us to dwell rather upon its splendour and helpfulness in the hours of its efficacy, to think how vast is then the expanse of waters which it illuminates, and its radiance how stèady and serene.

THE END.

For EU product safety concerns, contact us at Calle de José Abascal, 56–1°, 28003 Madrid, Spain or eugpsr@cambridge.org.

www.ingramcontent.com/pod-product-compliance
Ingram Content Group UK Ltd.
Pitfield, Milton Keynes, MK11 3LW, UK
UKHW010336140625
459647UK00010B/631